Repeat Printed Pattern
for Interiors

BLOOMSBURY VISUAL ARTS
Bloomsbury Publishing Plc
50 Bedford Square, London, WC1B 3DP, UK
1385 Broadway, New York, NY 10018, USA
29 Earlsfort Terrace, Dublin 2, Ireland

BLOOMSBURY, BLOOMSBURY VISUAL ARTS and the Diana logo are
trademarks of Bloomsbury Publishing Plc

First published in Great Britain 2023

Cover design: Adriana Brioso
Cover image *Bloomsbury Garden* in teal © Timorous Beasties

A catalogue record for this book is available from the British Library.

A catalogue record for this book is available from the Library of Congress.

ISBN: HB: 978-1-3501-2744-9
         PB: 978-1-3501-2740-1
       ePDF: 978-1-3501-2742-5
      eBook: 978-1-3501-2743-2

Typeset by Integra Software Services Pvt. Ltd.
Printed and bound in India

To find out more about our authors and books visit www.bloomsbury.com
and sign up for our newsletters.

Repeat Printed Pattern for Interiors

Kate Farley

BLOOMSBURY VISUAL ARTS
LONDON • NEW YORK • OXFORD • NEW DELHI • SYDNEY

CONTENTS

ABOUT THE AUTHOR

Kate Farley combines her design practice with an academic career. She is currently Associate Professor in Design at Norwich University of the Arts, leading the undergraduate courses of Fashion and Textile Design. She is a Senior Fellow of the Higher Education Academy, recognizing the sustained impact she has made on teaching and learning at undergraduate level.

With twenty-five years of design experience, Kate's practice focuses on bespoke and site-specific projects. Clients include Birmingham Airport, Barbican Centre London, Queen Elizabeth University Hospital Birmingham and David Mellor Design, with design commissions for exterior and interior surfaces and giftware, as well as fashion prints for Japanese brand, Stamp and Diary. Illustration projects include designing posters for Transport for London, limited edition prints for London Transport Museum, and the book, *Gardening with Mr Bawden*, for publisher Design for Today. Her bookworks are held in collections worldwide, including Tate Britain, the British Library, and Yale Center for British Arts, USA.

Kate has launched three collections under her own brand (*Plot to Plate* in 2012, *Construct* in 2015 and *Threads* in 2016), working with British manufacturers including Formica and Window Film Company, showcasing collections at trade shows.

Kate's academic research explores visual communication through pattern structures and addresses brand identity through pattern. She combines practical studio-based research with written papers.

Kate holds a BA Hons degree in Printed Textiles Design from Leeds College of Art and Design and an MA in Book Arts from Camberwell College of Arts.

Kate Farley

INTRODUCTION

This book celebrates repeating pattern, with the aim of raising awareness and understanding of the complex design processes and considerations involved in creating pattern today. Although the context of pattern in this book is for interiors, much of the design thinking is applicable when designing for alternative contexts such as fashion.

We can learn from what has gone before, to create our own relationship with pattern. Patterns and colour seep into our subconscious in our early days, influencing our personal relationship with the world we live in. Patterns affect our emotions, build memories and shape experiences. In the private spaces of our homes, we can use pattern to reflect our past, present and future aspirations. The examples in this book celebrate the skill of pattern building and the seduction of repetition.

The book begins by introducing the modern history of pattern in relation to the times those patterns were created, to underpin contemporary understanding of the subject and provide an overview of the language of pattern. The second chapter describes numerous contemporary approaches to creating repeating patterns for interior spaces, aiming to inform, inspire and support those wishing to understand the pattern design process. Designers working today have kindly shared their working methods and professional concerns, illustrating both traditional and digital practices, enabling us to fill the surfaces of our lives with pattern, to calm and soothe, as well as excite and inspire us. Pattern design sits alongside other exciting subjects in the creative industries, including trend research, manufacturing, market awareness and sustainability, but boundaries have had to be drawn to maintain the focus and intent of this book. This book can be a stepping-off point for further reading.

Each pattern in the book documents and illustrates different elements in the construction of motifs, building rhythms and repeating compositions. The book fills a gap in the market, working alongside the many instructional books available, by providing thorough design thinking and intent, beyond the how-to, as a valuable resource to inform you of what it takes to design strong patterns.

Why I make pattern

I vividly recall the patterns of my childhood: the orange geometric laminate in my grandma's kitchen, the stylized florals of my Clothkits dresses and the graphic micro pattern on the reverse of playing cards. They didn't turn me into a pattern designer, but they shaped my relationship with pattern language.

As a child, I loved colouring in isometric paper to create my own patterns and, while studying for my A-levels, I was encouraged to think about designing patterns for products—mainly socks, for some reason. At art school, initially in Norfolk and subsequently on my degree course in Printed Textile Design at Leeds College of Art and Design, I found that relief printing, along with screen printing, enabled me to create repeating rhythms. It was a discovery that showed me how multiple images could seduce in a way a single motif could not.

I set up my business, Kate Farley, in 1999 and since then have designed pattern for many surface materials and contexts, including artists' books, an airport terminal, public toilets, wallpapers and laminates. With each new venture there is excitement as motifs become compositions and patterns take shape, flowing across the sheet, screen or cloth, with rhythms demanding attention. Awkward edges and clumsy lines are refined and honed until the balance and harmony of resolution hold. I relish the troubleshooting of a complex composition and enjoy the challenge of creating pattern that feels familiar and comfortable, yet offers a new take on an old pattern structure. There is an art to problem-solving pattern and my benchmark of design heroes is set high: Josef Frank, Enid Marx and Lucienne Day, to name three.

A pattern designer does not invent the mechanics of repetition, but works with visual rhythms and original ingredients, building on the traditions of pattern construction. I am driven by the challenge of visually communicating information through pattern and really enjoy making a pattern work the best it can in an efficient, articulate form.

Deconstructing a pattern: The making of Hanbury

I am taking you through my design process for creating the pattern **Hanbury**, to demonstrate the many decisions I made along the way. I have chosen this particular pattern as it is fairly complex, with many different elements to it, including large and small motifs that work together to provide balance, rhythmic variation, visual interest and decoration.

My aim was to create a design based on a traditional pattern structure. My inspiration was a flocked wallpaper containing circular interlocking motifs I had seen at Hanbury Hall, a National Trust property in Worcestershire, England. I was keen to create a decorative, more detailed pattern from my previous patterns to demonstrate my versatility as a designer.

At the time, I was creating my *Plot to Plate* pattern collection inspired by allotments and vegetable plots, but I wanted to include formal

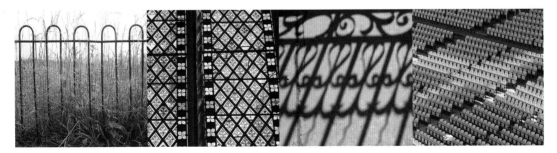

Figure 0.1 Patterns out and about.

gardens, making a link between traditional garden design and textile design. I sketched flower borders as well as kitchen gardens to generate motifs and inform composition and rhythms. I did not want to create a pattern that was recognizable as a garden, with obvious flowers and borders, but rather an interpretation.

I began by creating diagrams investigating the circular structure with the motifs I had drawn, building up areas of detail alongside textured micro patterns in my sketchbook. I initially focused on designing a tile of one full circle and four quarter circles that could be repeated to create larger areas of pattern.

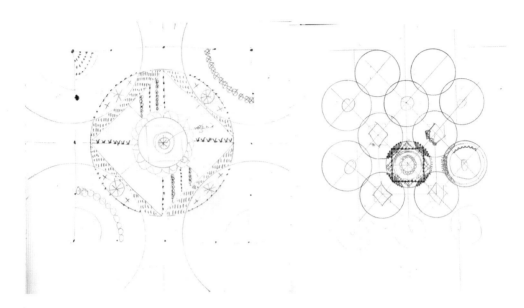

Figure 0.2 Initial design idea.

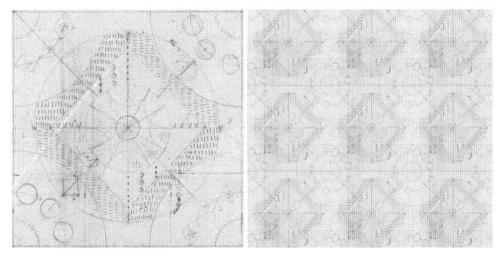

Figure 0.3 First draft and scanned artwork.

Once I had developed the first draft of the pattern, I scanned the artwork and roughly placed it in a full-drop repeat to get a sense of scale in the motifs, and the overall visual rhythms.

I planned to use lino printing to create the visual language of the pattern as I had done in previous patterns in the *Plot to Plate* collection. Although linocutting can create a textural quality, I wanted to use it for the clean graphic quality it would give the motifs, referencing back to the clean flocked motifs at Hanbury Hall. I cut the lino block and printed the first iteration of the design, scanning the black on white print to once again test the repeating rhythms digitally.

There were elements that stood out as unsatisfactory, particularly the petal-like motifs around the four quarter circles; once in repeat they were too obvious in comparison with the other details. I decided to make them smaller and add more to reduce the impact of each one.

I wanted to add greater variation by adding more patterned texture so I removed one of the circular motifs and replaced it with a rectangular form set inside a large circle. I also added more visual texture in small micro patterns. I created larger repeating areas of both new developments digitally to check the growing rhythm. Both patterns felt too noisy and stilted, with some

Figure 0.4 Lino printing.

Figure 0.5 Repeat rhythms.

areas appearing too dominant. The pattern was lacking finesse and satisfactory detail.

Sometimes while working on the computer, ideas appear that are unexpected but worth exploring further. The patterns in Figure 0.6 played with connecting the circular motifs as waves. They felt reminiscent of the Art Deco period, and after a little design development I realized it was not quite what I was after, so I abandoned that direction.

Figure 0.6 Circular motifs as waves.

Figure 0.7 Motif details.

When I design, I tend to create artwork using drawing or printmaking, then scan the motifs to further manipulate the design digitally. This image shows some individual motifs I moved about in Adobe Photoshop to test the details of the design. I also use guides to ensure the alignment of motifs, as in a geometric design any misplaced motif may appear more obvious when repeated across a large wall. I only tidy up and clean small details of my lino printing as I don't want it to appear too precise; otherwise I could have created an accurate graphic pattern using Adobe Illustrator. There are signs of irregularity in the hand-cut artwork to make it clear it came from a lino print.

I had to consider the manufacturing processes available for wallpaper printing, and wanted something more traditional than digital printing. I chose flexographic printing, which works as a relief print method, suiting the aesthetic of my artwork. The process involves printing from a circular cylinder holding the raised artwork, so the design needs to be 52 cm wide for the standard width of wallpaper, and the circumference of the roller was 53 cm, therefore determining the repeat tile size. There would be a ground colour applied, then the single-coloured pattern printed. With this knowledge I could ensure all artwork met the manufacturer's specification as I progressed.

Although it took me a while to place all the star-like motifs and repeat the tile in the versions shown in Figure 0.8, the overall pattern felt too fussy, so I removed some of those motifs.

Figures 0.8–0.9 Star-like motif and different colourway.

Figure 0.10 a–b Testing the inclusion of the hexagonal motif for added variation.

I wanted to create a pattern with a little more gravitas. I test the design in different colourways (as shown in Figure 0.9) as I go, to see how the motifs look. Scale and weight of motifs, as well as relationships between motifs, can control the spirit of the pattern.

The two tiles shown in Figures 0.10 a and b appear very similar on first sight, but by swapping out two of the circles and adding hexagons as alternating motifs in the right-hand version (b), the design holds much more interest and the repeating tile is larger. The hexagon provides more dynamism with the straight edges in contrast to all the circles. They would alternate across the design, altering the overall rhythm.

This was an exciting development that resulted in a more interesting repeating composition. I had created this new shape by linocutting

a new motif, and scanning the print in the same way as all the other motifs, so it belonged with the rest. The dotted crossed lines within the hexagon linked to the dots in the central circular motif on a diagonal axis to lead the eye from motif to motif. I removed the horizontal row of Vs and added vertical curves, again to lead the eye from shape to shape and increase variation in the pattern. In the middle of the larger circular forms, I swapped every other central motif to include one with a lighter background in contrast to the existing darker one. This is a tiny detail, but adds visual interest and results in a larger repeating tile.

It is important to test a pattern to see how it flows across a large area if designing for interior surfaces. I printed the pattern at full-scale and lived with it in the studio to see how details and overall pattern repeat appeared as I grew more familiar with it over time. I tested colours by painting gouache swatches and looked at them under various lighting conditions at different times of day and night. I had to specify the ground colour and the printed colour for manufacturing, and sent the printer the paint swatches as well as Pantone references. The final wallpaper has a calm pale-blue base colour, over-printed with a chalky teal colour.

Figures 0.11–12 Full-scale test and gouache swatches.

Figure 0.13 Final design, Hanbury.

GRAMMAR OF ORNAMENT.

PLATE

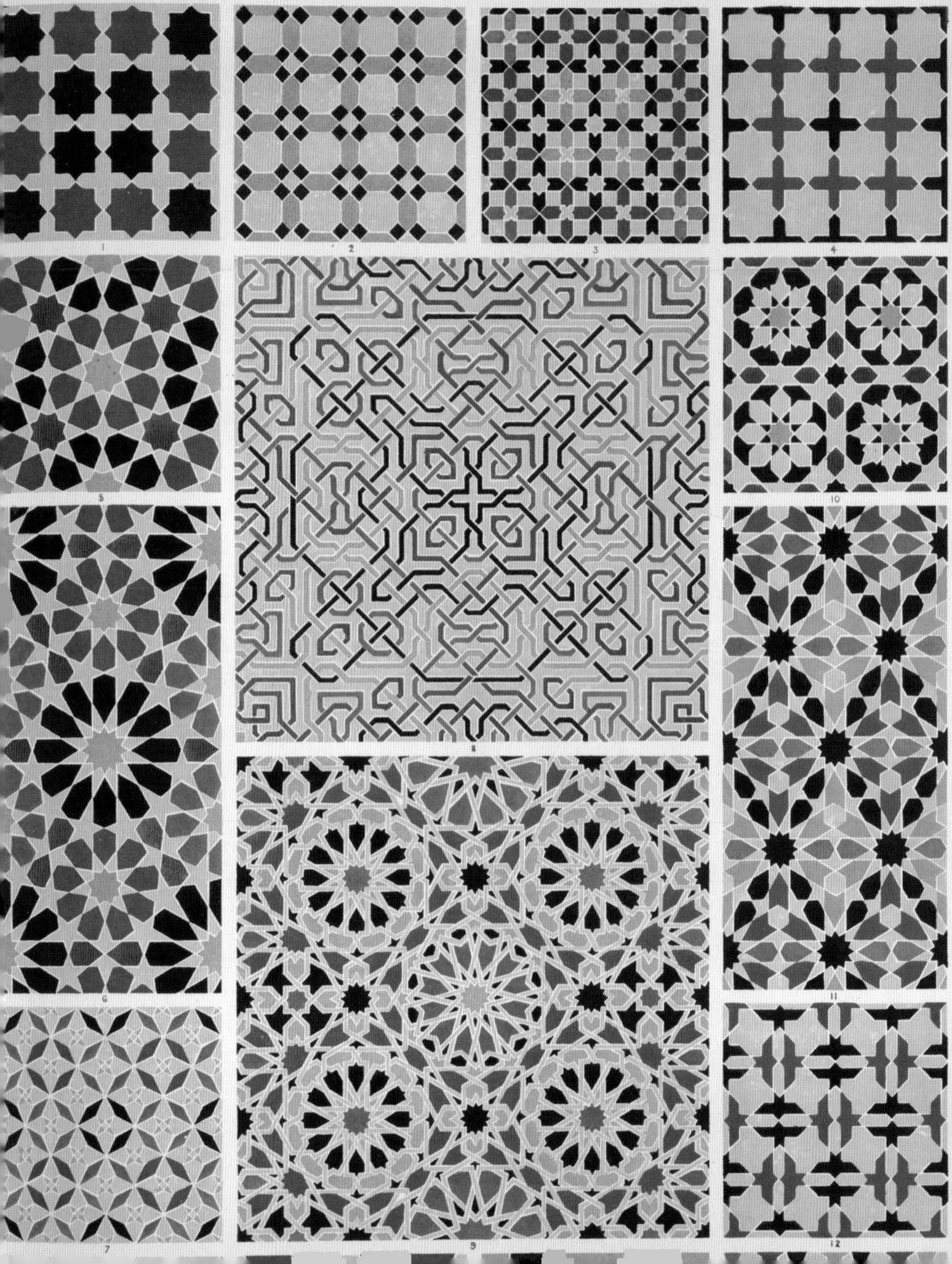

1

Patterns in History

Introduction

The purpose of this chapter is to outline key developments of pattern for interiors in relation to social, cultural, political and technological factors, in order to inform contemporary understanding.

Patterns for textiles can hold unique national and geographical identities, shaped by factors including traditions of craft processes, historic motifs and social customs. Textile processes, colour and stylized imagery can communicate the provenance of a pattern to the rest of the world. Woven Kente cloth of Ghana and indigo-dyed tsutugaki cloth from Japan are good examples of this. Traditions of weaving, printing and dyeing exist on all continents in some form, shaped by local raw materials and craft practices.

Figure 1.1 This page, labelled 'Moresque No. 5' from *The Grammar of Ornament*, illustrates strong and striking geometric patterns and shows Owen Jones' (1809–1874) interests in recording pattern designs from international sources.

It was not until industrialization that printed pattern became available on a commercial scale for the domestic market. Reflecting on factors relevant to designers of pattern today, the period covered begins at the close of the eighteenth century.

For centuries the textile industry has developed across international boundaries, trading raw materials, sharing technical innovations, inspiring design aesthetics and consumer tastes. Trade across Asia, through to Europe, demonstrates the international journey of raw materials, and illustrates how the patterns of India and the Middle East have inspired textiles manufactured in Britain. Included are European influences from Ancient Greeks and Romans on nineteenth-century pattern, via the evolution of European Modernism, through to the present day. To move forward in design, the past provides inspiration and reassurance. By learning from what has gone before, pattern designers reinterpret historic pattern languages for contemporary audiences.

During this period, Britain has sold textiles worldwide and competed with France for dominance of the international luxury textiles market. Britain has returned many times to the debate surrounding quality versus mass-produced cheaper cloth. This chapter features designers embracing craft processes as well as those championing technologies, and shows how twenty-first-century digital processes are providing new ways to create and manufacture patterns.

This chapter predominantly features patterns in a European and British context, providing a concise narrative of design evolution, referencing recurring pattern themes and interrelated networks of designers within the last 300 years.

Patterns in history

Early history and its influence: Making pattern has been a human activity for thousands of years; on cave walls, as marks in the sand, and as part of home decoration and clothing. Some of these patterns have repeatedly influenced generations of designers. Looking for and finding the relationships and developments of ancient patterns is fascinating and can illustrate how connected the world of pattern is to international trade, education, social events and the environment. Contemporary designers can use their knowledge of historic patterns by interpreting them for the current age; creating a new legacy as an archive of today as well as a link with pattern history. By understanding the ingredients of successful pattern, we can communicate historic references or challenge convention in our own artwork.

Why do patterns look as they do? Factors such as tradition, craft skills, science and technology, historic style and taste, international trade and cultural context influence pattern. Influencing the way the artwork looks, designs could be in celebration of an international event (such as the discovery of the tomb of Tutankhamun in

Egypt), or made possible due to technological innovations of the time (such as screen printing). There are some subjects, such as florals, that never go out of fashion but the way the imagery is stylized or composed often reflects prevailing style.

Styles of art, design or music do not start and finish cleanly at the end of a decade just to make it easy to remember. Styles evolve and come in and out of fashion and tastes change; styles merge, run parallel and can last longer in some countries than others. Often a new style is a reaction to an old one, attempting a break from what has gone before. There may be an early-adopter period of a new style or art movement, then momentum gathers with more general acceptance. Gradually, the new style will wane and signs of a new taste may develop. It is valuable to see what is happening across the creative disciplines to note how styles translate between architecture, fine art and music, as pattern design may well be taking influence from or influencing these other contexts.

The next section introduces key design periods in modern history, illustrating how styles of printed pattern have evolved in relation to their contexts. In illustrating particular styles, some of the selected examples of pattern for interiors have been woven but contain strong examples of stylizing motifs and compositions equally applicable to printed textiles.

Baroque bold 1700s–1850s

From the seventeenth century through to the mid-eighteenth century the Baroque style dominated, and later continued as a popular style, shaping architecture, music, dance, painting and wider cultural contexts predominantly across Europe and to some extent across the world, becoming one of the earliest international styles. Flamboyant, dramatic and highly decorative in style, public buildings including theatres and churches were ornately adorned with stone swags of carved cloth, highly detailed bouquets of flowers, angels, cherubs and animals. London's St Paul's Cathedral and the Palace of Versailles in France epitomize the Baroque style in architecture while composers such as Vivaldi and Handel musically evoke the Baroque style, expressing dynamism and emotion, inducing a sense of awe and wonder.

For interior and pattern design this was a period of overindulgence—for those who could afford it. Setting the tone for the home, wallpaper and heavy draped curtains were accompanied by ornately carved wooden furniture. Frequently bold and deep in colour, these interiors were not for the shy and retiring. Flocked wallpapers, with the pattern created in raised fibres stuck to the surface, provided cheaper alternatives to expensive velvet hangings. The patterns were often large in scale with symmetrical floral flourishes, although some were less structured repeats with flowing florals, possibly easier to use in smaller rooms. The Baroque style informed the Rococo style emerging from France, a comparatively toned down and more light-hearted decorative style.

Figure 1.3 This French woven silk furnishing fabric from 1850 illustrates the Rococo style, with the floral motifs contained by asymmetrical scrolls (details found on architectural ornamentation and furniture of the period). The contrasting hues of gold and blue thread provide an interesting interplay of negative and positive space. The French textiles industry, centred around Lyon, produced fine silk weaves—a status symbol amongst the wealthy aristocrats.

Figure 1.2 This mid-nineteenth-century sample of French jacquard woven silk fabric is an example of two-tone stylized natural forms in the Baroque style. The jacquard loom, invented in France at the turn of the nineteenth century, enables ornate pattern cloth to be woven. This sample typifies the designs that could also be seen on flocked wallpapers and printed cloth.

The Baroque style was not universally popular. Being seen as indulgent and excessive by critics, there were also concerns that the ornate nature of the furniture and excess of fabrics could result in more germs in the home. A less ornate style was seen by some as healthier and more desirable, paving the way for a Classical revival.

Neoclassical formality 1750s–1810s

A good example of design tastes changing is the shift from the Baroque style to the Classical Revival across Europe from the mid-eighteenth century through to the beginning of the nineteenth century. After the frivolity of the Baroque period, proponents of the new style adopted a more serious tone. Borrowing from ancient Greece and Rome, they advocated a sense of order, symmetry and classical storytelling and made use of mathematical principles to achieve order in design and a measured rationale.

Aristocratic young gentlemen travelled across Europe on study tours in what became known as the Grand Tour. Readying them for employment, this rite of passage became their finishing school. The design principles of key design influencers such as Owen Jones (1809–74) and Christopher Dresser (1834–1904) were both significantly affected by this opportunity.

It was common for these young men to bring back artefacts from their travels and interest in classical objects grew. Thomas Hope (1769–1831), a young Dutch designer and considerable collector from Greece, Egypt and beyond, introduced Britain to the concept of interior decoration

Figure 1.4 This pictorial pattern, *Les monuments d'Égypte* from the early nineteenth century, printed in a monochromatic palette by leading French manufacturers Oberkampf, features Egyptian landmarks and icons, picking up on the French public's interest in Egypt at the time, following Napoleon Bonaparte's (1769–1821) tour of the region. The design uses the formality of the grid in the background with stylized lotus flower at the intersections to support the well-spaced larger floating motifs on top, including the striking pyramid motifs alongside more textural foliage. The eye is drawn to the large motifs initially but finds visual interest across the design.

Figure 1.5 Despite this woven design (*Italian*) being a later design in Owen Jones' career, it was undoubtedly inspired by his international travel. The balance of two key motifs, one larger and slightly bolder than the other, creates a sense of depth between imagery and background. The lighter line running through the centre of the bold leaves creates an ogee S shape through the design.

with his book *Household Furniture and Interior Decoration* (1807). He encouraged a return to a classical approach to design, an aim supported by architect Robert Adam (1728–92), who believed building interiors should be in keeping with the exterior scheme. The neoclassical period saw architectural features—columns, pediments and porticoes—influencing the interior design of buildings in features such as marble-effect paint

Figure 1.6 This example includes classical columns arranged within small scenes, reminiscent of the French *toile de Jouy* fabrics, but produced in Britain (*c*. 1770, manufactured by John Munns). Utilizing single colour on a pale cloth, a dominant view of columns and arches is balanced by a smaller-scale view of trees and an urn. Foliage creates movement and rhythm across the design, connecting the larger elements.

work, fresco-inspired surface pattern and draped lightweight fabrics.

From the fifteenth century, Italy and France had both established significant textiles manufacturing abilities, importing raw materials and competing for the European luxury market with woven cloth such as patterned silk velvets for the formal interiors of the day, as well as fabrics for fashion markets. France was keen to develop existing craft practices, including spinning, dyeing and printing, to enable more reliable production. Oberkampf, established by Christophe-Philippe Oberkampf (1738–1815), was one of the key manufacturers in France, and a good example of a company making the shift from block printing to cylindrical metal plate printing, enabling rapid printing of repeating designs.

The company Oberkampf is renowned for the *toile du Jouy* designs of pictorial scenes. It is a historic pattern design style (within European design) that continues to be utilized by designers today. The *toile du Jouy* cloth would traditionally be made of woven cotton with a white or off-white base colour featuring single-colour printed images of small scenes.

Trading with pattern (*chintz and paisley*) 1680s–1830s

International trade as far back as before the Greek Empire had enabled the sharing of design influences between cultures. Along formal trading routes between India and Europe, including the Silk Route, products such as tea, spices and cloth were imported to Europe into the eighteenth century. Chintz, a glazed cotton fabric imported from India that features floral patterns, often printed on pale backgrounds, was much admired, becoming extremely sought after in

Europe. From the 1680s the increasing desirability of chintz resulted in a ban on its import to Europe, as it threatened the French and British textile industries. To satisfy consumer demand, British manufacturers produced designs similar in style to these imported fabrics.

As well as chintz, items such as carpets and shawls were traded along the Silk Route and sold to Europeans as luxury gifts with the allure of exotic, faraway lands. These items often featured traditional regional motifs, including the teardrop *boteh* or *buta*, arranged along borders around the edges of scarves and rugs as well as in non-repeating designs. Another example of British

Figure 1.7 This British printed textile design, heavily inspired by the traditional chintz fabric from India and surrounding countries, was manufactured by Bannister Hall, one of the leading firms for woodblock chintzes. The typical cream background supports stylized floral sprigs over-printed in several shades of colour marking out detail and structure of flowers and leaves. Stems are printed with darker outlines to create a flowing web across the pattern, leading the eye between key motifs. This design makes good use of scale, offering a variety of motifs and rhythms between small sprigs and buds, alongside larger flower heads in more dominant colours.

Figure 1.8 This woven wall hanging (*c.* 1820), attributed to Kashmir, India, is a good example of the *buta* motif in a border pattern, surrounding a placement design of a tree and surrounding foliage. Typically featuring deep reds, blues and greens, these designs are often extremely intricate with pattern detail filling in the negative shape as well as the positive motifs.

markets cashing in on popular foreign styles is found in Paisley, Scotland where the established textile industry responded to the demand for the exotic by manufacturing highly patterned decorative textiles. This cloth, featuring the *buta* teardrop motif, came to be known as paisley pattern among British consumers; shawls featuring the design were eventually printed rather than woven to speed up production and reduce costs. This pattern has had international reach and is continually revived for both fashion and interiors markets.

With the growing international exploration of the time, patterns and motifs were gathered by designers. It was common for Greek, Egyptian and Middle Eastern-inspired ornamentation to be featured in architecture of this era as well as on household items such as ceramics, wallpapers, textiles and furniture.

Gothic rules 1830s–1860s

Truth was the order of the day amongst the advocates of the next reinvention in British design: the Gothic Revival of the mid-nineteenth century embraces medieval aesthetic and celebrates purity, honesty and craftsmanship. The approach

Figure 1.9 The striped pattern from the eighteenth century showcases an international mix of motifs, from the Greek key design in blue, to the Indian *buta*-shape paisley. The pattern switches between the formal stripe of the blue geometric motif to the fluid and flowing paisley motif, demonstrating increasingly eclectic influences of the designers through their growing awareness of other cultural styles and motifs.

was driven in particular by architect, theorist and designer Augustus Pugin (1812–52) and artist, critic and thinker, John Ruskin (1819–1900). Both men considered design to be crucial to wellbeing, and good design was a moral responsibility to society. Pugin demanded 'truth to materials' rather than neoclassical trends such as painting marble effects and imitation wood grain on walls in place of genuine marble or wood.

They also objected to the neoclassical designs featuring buildings and fictional landscapes (as in *toiles du Jouy*) and the implication that the views were outside the window of the room in which they were hung. Pugin and Ruskin advocated that if there was to be any pattern on walls it should be flat, graphic and not deceitful.

Pugin designed many churches as well as contributing significantly to the rebuild of

Figure 1.10a This design by Pugin demonstrates his fascination with ecclesiastical architectural detailing and his desire to create flat patterns in formal structured compositions. He has interpreted the subject of stained glass as an organized, almost diagrammatic design, providing a striped design with half-drop repeating arched details. This repeating structure provides the alternating diagonal effect.

Figure 1.10b This detail of the previous image illustrates Pugin's attention to detail, designing large-scale formal compositions with ornate detail to provide visual interest. This is particularly useful if a surface design is for a large interior space, enabling the pattern to work at varying distances from the viewer.

London's Houses of Parliament alongside lead architect Charles Barry (1795–1860). Pugin took responsibility for designing the majority of surface patterns for the interior, including floor tiles, wallpapers and textile designs. In his quest for truth, Pugin employed heavily stylized floral forms and graphic motifs to create an ordered pattern of clean outlines and bright colours.

An 1836 parliamentary select committee on Arts and Manufacturers raised concerns that manufactured goods in Britain were too often of poor design quality, due to the rising pace of the export race, damaging the nation's reputation as design leaders. As a result, in 1837, Government Schools of

Design were established with the aims of promoting the benefits of good design, educating people in good taste, increasing profit and re-establishing Britain's design reputation. To achieve this ambition, design inspiration, production processes and use of historic references were taught.

Pugin inspired a generation of younger designers looking to develop their careers. Christopher Dresser, having been a student on the Government Schools scheme, could see the merits of a Gothic revival. Dresser developed stylized motifs (such as exotic birds, fans and delicate plants) in the Gothic Revival spirit with links to geometric structures, for tiles, ceramic tableware, metalware,

Figure 1.11 From 1883, this later artwork by Christopher Dresser demonstrates a very clean graphic style of pattern design using bold colours and incorporating flat shapes, symmetrical motifs and stylized lines approved of by Pugin. This design drawing may well be for a larger repeating design or tile for an interior context and has been painted using graphite, ink and gouache paints.

furniture and textiles. Unlike Ruskin and Pugin, however, Dresser embraced modern methods of industrial design and manufacturing to increase production of items of ceramics and metalware.

In 1851 Britain hosted the Great Exhibition, an international fair held in London, established by Queen Victoria's husband, Prince Albert, with the aim of presenting Britain as the superpower of industrialization and building international trading networks. Supporters believed Britain proved its position as world leader, but critics were quick to state that more work was needed in improving design skills while increasing manufacturing capabilities.

In 1856 architect and design reformer Owen Jones published *The Grammar of Ornament,* a folio of highly patterned illustrations providing an invaluable design source of flat pattern for those not privileged to see all that he had seen on his Grand Tour. The book includes patterns, borders, geometric repeats, florals and motifs from across the world, in clear and stylized form, enabling the reader to identify key characteristics of decorative work from around the globe. Lavishly produced, it was designed not for the purpose of copying and imitating the patterns, but to inform designers of the basic tools of the trade, and to show options for seeing and designing pattern for the modern world. Jones, particularly influenced by surface decoration he found in Spain and Africa, also presented lectures and published articles on his idea of good design.

Jones was admired for his commitment, but his critics argued that the patterns became diminished through presentation outside of their original cultural context; they lacked reference to the distinctiveness of their history, geography, religion and culture. Concerns about cultural appropriation continue today and designers need to be mindful of this when referencing others' cultures.

Figure 1.12 This page from Owen Jones' *The Grammar of Ornament* showcases the stylized botanical forms encouraged by Jones and other design teachers of the time. Flat diagrammatic flowers and leaves are displayed to educate a designer in how to look and interpret the popular subject of nature in surface decoration.

Arts and Crafts and the Aesthetic agenda, 1860s–1890s

The Arts and Crafts movement of the second half of the nineteenth century borrowed from medieval influences, not only in the imagery inspired by the Gothic Revival, but also in craft practices and production. Designs for churches and private commissions established the portfolio of clients.

One of the most influential designers with an international reputation for retrospectively defining this period is William Morris (1834–96) and his company Morris & Co. The company celebrated nature and beauty through colourful and striking repeat patterns of flora and fauna flowing across walls, floors, ceramics and upholstery. Notable designers and artists worked for Morris & Co., including the Pre-Raphaelite artists Edward Burne-Jones (1833–98) and Dante Gabriel Rossetti (1828–82).

Morris worked with leading textile manufacturer Thomas Wardle (1831–1909) to develop a natural dye and print workshop using traditional techniques, shunning quicker and easier modern processes. The impact of increased industrialization on the quality of products was a significant concern for Morris; he believed that objects made by hand would be appreciated more by the consumer. However, handmade items were far more costly than mass-produced ones, making them unaffordable for most people. Also, at this time Guilds of Handicrafts were being established across Britain to sustain creative livelihoods by attracting consumers who would appreciate and could afford handmade objects.

Morris's skill as a pattern designer ranged across print, weave, embroidery and non-textile applications, but all in a style recognized as Arts and Crafts. With motifs regularly built on traditional pattern structures such as the ogee and trellis and often featuring dramatic variations in scales of detail (with dominant flower heads, trailing foliage and infilling of motifs as smaller elements including leaves and flowers) many of Morris's designs show a love of the traditional English garden. However, Morris's well-travelled colleague Henry Dearle (1859–1932) brought

Figure 1.13a *Honeysuckle*, designed by William Morris in 1876 and printed by Morris & Co., demonstrates Morris's ability to design complex patterns following formal structure. This design employs an ogee composition, with the widening and narrowing circular structure created by an 'S' shaping the placement of flower heads and stems in a vertical stripe. The symmetry and balance of the design is being provided by mirroring motifs.

Figure 1.13b This detail of the Honeysuckle design by William Morris shows the over-printing of each block to build the design, using line and flat printed colour. Morris's printing blocks would be time-consuming to create, therefore expensive, so attention to detail for each block was vital.

Figure 1.14 Morris's woven design, *Violet and Columbine*, was registered to Morris & Co. in the 1880s. The design shows a different use of elements; there is less variation in scale across the motifs, but it is colour that defines one motif from another. Horizontal stripes of blue and orange flower heads create clarity in the composition, highlighted against the green foliage that provides a relatively even visual texture across the composition.

Figure 1.15 *Ispahan* was designed by Henry Dearle in 1888 and woven in wool for Morris & Co. This ogee pattern features arches linking larger stylized flower heads. Within this composition smaller details are made up of leaves and the motifs are flat representations of plants in tonal hues. Some of the motifs are given a halo effect in the colour choice, lifting them above the dark ground and tonal horizontal stripes to further the visual interest and depth. This design is sometimes attributed to Morris and demonstrates the complexity of a design company led by the key figure of Morris, yet relying on collaboration and inspiration from others. Dearle became Art Director following Morris's death in 1896.

his interest of traditional patterns of Asia to the design studio, reflecting the international design language gaining in popularity at this time.

The Aesthetic movement was running in parallel with the Arts and Crafts movement in the latter half of the nineteenth century in Britain. With the directive of 'art for art's sake', artists, writers and designers adopting the Aesthetic approach were challenging the increasing industrialization and conservative expectations of formal Victorian society, preferring self-expression and beauty as the drivers for their creative progress. In fashion, the Aesthetic style encouraged free-draping garments rather than the restrictive items more usually worn by Victorian women. The Aesthetic style celebrates art objects and handcrafted products, with nature as the overriding theme (birds and plants familiar to an English garden as well as exotic specimens from Japan), visual qualities that would inform the incoming Art Nouveau style.

Liberty & Co. Ltd (Liberty) was a significant retailer established during the height of the Arts and Crafts movement in 1875. The store showcased international exotic products such as carpets, vases and curiosities alongside British designs on a range of products, both for fashion and interiors. It strove to provide new and different products from its competitors.

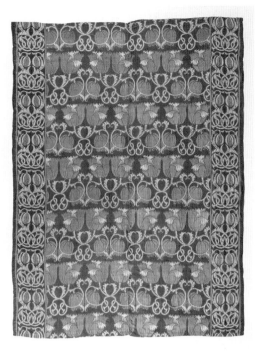

Figure 1.16 Peacock feathers were popular symbols in the Aesthetic movement, with feathers used for accessories and as motifs for textiles and surface pattern. This design, *Hera*, from 1887, named after the Greek goddess, is attributed to Arthur Silver of Silver Studio and sold through Liberty, although there is evidence to suggest Christopher Dresser may have been the designer. First issued as a woven design, it was subsequently roller printed rather than woodblock printed, roller printing being a more economical production method at this time. The design was relaunched by Liberty for the company's exhibition at the Victoria and Albert Museum, London, in 1975 (a time of interest in the Aesthetic designs of Victorian Britain) and has become one of the brand's most recognizable patterns for furnishing and fashion fabrics.

Figure 1.17 This block-printed bedcover designed by Charles Voysey in 1888 for British textiles company GP & J Baker typifies the continuing Eastern influence European designers embraced at this time. The design features stylized forms inspired by chintz florals, echoed through the border design made up of smaller-scale pattern using the same motifs. The blue ground with orange key motifs is a common colour combination of the period, employing harmonious complementary colours of blue and orange.

During this period, it was not uncommon for architects to design for other contexts, and like Augustus Pugin, architect Charles F. A. Voysey (1857–1941) designed patterns and furniture too. Considered one of the key Arts and Crafts designers, Voysey believed in high-quality materials, evolving a design practice that flowed seamlessly from Arts and Crafts, through to the Art Nouveau style, selling through retailer Liberty and working with notable manufacturers (including Alexander Morton & Co., Essex & Co. and Jeffrey & Co. printers). With striking simplicity, sparing backgrounds and elegance in his stylized motifs and attractive rhythms, Voysey's flat patterns were less complex than those of Morris. His passion for the natural world is reflected in the many patterns incorporating motifs of animals, flowers and birds. Voysey sustained a highly regarded design career well into the twentieth century.

Art Nouveau and the decorative style 1890s–1930s

The London-based department store Liberty was perfect for those continuing to embrace the Aesthetic style and appreciation for well-crafted goods of the Arts and Crafts movement, but was also forward-thinking in embracing the modern style, sometimes referred to as Liberty style, referencing the company as style-setter. Designers such as Archibold Knox (1864–1933), William Morris, Lindsay Phillip Butterfield (1869–1948) and Charles Voysey were an excellent match for this

store. Liberty was buying designs and outsourcing production, so designs are often attributed to the retailer rather than the individual designer.

The anticipation of the turn of the century saw designers and their patrons looking to embrace new design inspiration. There was a passion at this time for design without historical reference, but it is difficult to forget history completely as almost any pattern structure is likely to build on what has gone before. The new style, therefore, while dynamic and modern in its use of decoration, was at times reminiscent of Romanticism and Aestheticism as well as 'exotic' stylization inspired by international references from India and Japan. Albeit with some national

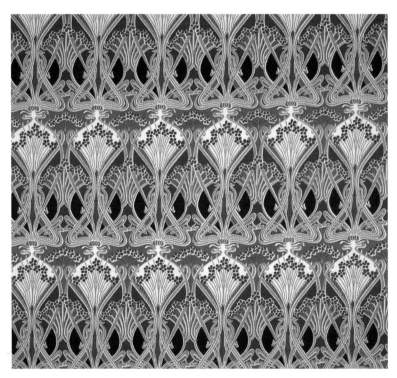

Figure 1.18 The French Art Nouveau designer René Beauclair (1877–1960) created this design before it was redrawn by David Haward's Studio for Liberty in 1902. The title, *Ianthe* (violet flower), suggests this pattern may originate from floral forms but, as was typical for Art Nouveau motifs, lines are stretched and forms simplified, with angular curves contouring across the design. The design has since been issued on other fabrics and scarves by Liberty.

differences, the Art Nouveau style spread across Europe, peaking with the 1900 Paris Exposition, which brought together examples of the style in glass, ceramics, textiles, furniture and the fine arts. The term Modern Style or *Style Moderne* also refers to this period.

Scottish architect Charles Rennie Mackintosh (1868–1928) generated a significant portfolio of patterns during this period, and his buildings and interior schemes continue to inform and inspire today. Mackintosh is considered to have been one of Britain's key designers of Art Nouveau pattern and he believed, in line with C. F. A. Voysey and Pugin before him, that a building's identity is formed by a connection between exterior and interior detail.

Pattern designs of the early twentieth century were optimistic and uplifting, using cheerful colour palettes and decorative motifs featuring fluid and feminine lines reminiscent of the still popular Aesthetic movement. European cities were embracing the spirit of Art Nouveau in architecture, the graphic arts and industrial design.

The ambition of the new style was to celebrate the decorative arts, breaking away from the previous academic conventions, rather than conforming to one style. Flowing and sweeping lines, swirls and dynamic rhythms translated across metalwork in the street, to small-scale fixtures and fittings in the domestic environment. There were highly decorative features across the disciplines of furniture, lighting and interiors, with a strong use of natural forms evolving from the Arts and Crafts style. Motifs were sometimes elongated, like dripping hot metal, weighted and poured. Birds were key subjects, combined with smaller details of curved and contouring geometric structures. European patterns were inspired by interest in the exoticism, elegance

Figure 1.19 *Poppies*, by freelance designer Lindsay Phillip Butterfield for Turnbull & Stockdale Ltd, demonstrates the popular style inspired by Japanese artwork, with multi-layered elegant flowing forms, and the graphic stylization of the motifs, inspired by woodblock printing. The background is barely visible but provides the impression we are looking through the poppies, adding depth to the pattern.

and grace of the Japanese aesthetic, seen as pure and untainted by consumerism.

Establishing the European agenda for design in this period, the decorative style in the early twentieth century, retrospectively termed Art Deco, took its cue from the 1925 International Exhibition of Modern Decorative and Industrial Arts in Paris. Delayed by the First World War, the Exhibition was a rather late acknowledgement of the design approach at this time. Stemming originally from the French luxury market and reinterpreted across Europe and America, the decorative aesthetic pulled stylistically from non-Western pattern (including from Africa and the Orient). Traditional Egyptian motifs were particularly popular following the discovery of the Tomb of Tutankhamun in 1922. Increased international travel resulted in materials considered exotic (such as ebony, ivory and lacquerware) becoming more accessible to European customers. Following the horrors of the First World War, interior decoration embraced glamour, luxury and escapism, with France particularly leading on opulence and ornamentation; Britain embraced the style with a more accessible, broad-market appeal.

This was a fast and furious era; a machine age of speeding engines, glamorous travel and the lively spirit of American jazz. Pattern was flat and stylized, with motifs of birds, plants and animals alongside dynamic geometric motifs. Diagonal stripes and propeller patterns shone in bright and metallic pride; rays of sunshine, sunbursts and dynamic curves exploded from designs. The influence of African patterns provided strong geometric statements, with printed circular motifs and zig-zags. Bright colour palettes, black outlines and metallics vied for the attention of consumers. Woodcarving, stained glass, enamelware, bookbinding, ceramics as well as textiles all featured vibrant pattern.

Figure 1.20 This pattern for furnishing fabric designed by Gregory F. Brown (1887–1948) and manufactured by leading English manufacturer William Foxton provides energy and three-dimensionality through looping and zig-zagging monochrome 'ribbons' providing the Art Deco spirit.

Art Deco carried well across the built environment, with architectural schemes and domestic interiors incorporating wall coverings, flooring and textiles in the style. This helped to provide a coherent look in any interior scheme, whether it be the royal yacht, the foyer of the Savoy hotel or a private lounge. Fine art paintings and sculptures were seen as decorative items in interior schemes. Following the First World War, new civic buildings across Europe were designed in this dynamic and optimistic style, with international designers embracing the opportunities to fulfil exciting large-scale schemes, while also embracing increasing opportunities to design for trains, cruise liners and aeroplanes.

Inspired by a fascination with celebrity lifestyles and the silver screen, 1930s' America saw a growing interest in interior design not only amongst the wealthy. Long-established brand Schumacher embraced the Art Deco style, providing rich woven and printed textiles. French fashion designer Paul Poiret provided European style for the brand, launching a spectacular pattern collection for fabric and wallpapers featuring designs with champagne bubbles, ostrich feathers, flowing ribbons, stylized florals and leaping deer. Following the Second World War, Schumacher continued collaborating with strong industry partners, including print designer Vera Neuman (1907–93), Italian-born Surrealist designer Elsa Schiaparelli (1890–1973) and Austrian émigré Josef Frank (1885–1967).

Artisan approach 1900s–1930s

Visual qualities within fine art practices frequently inform pattern design. The language of fine art at this time saw stylized and abstracted forms (e.g. Cubism, Futurism and Vorticism), inspiring designers to be braver in testing new expressive qualities of painting that suited draped fabrics for interiors as well as fashion applications. The groundbreaking style of Impressionism in Europe changed the way mark making could be understood with paint and colour as non-representational tones, but it was Post-Impressionism and artists such as Cézanne (1839–1906), Van Gogh (1853–1890) and Gauguin (1848–1903) that significantly shaped and gave confidence to European commercial pattern makers in the early twentieth century.

The continuing mechanization across the textile and wallpaper industry in Europe through the nineteenth century and into the twentieth century resulted in products getting to market faster and more cheaply; but there was a backlash, with critics once more blaming mechanization for a decrease in quality. If a machine could print more colours faster, was it right to do so? Was production capability driving the market instead of quality design?

Vienna embraced the creative energy of Art Nouveau, with artists such as Gustav Klimt (1862–1918) inspiring design contemporaries such as Joseph Urban (1872–1933) and Josef Hoffmann (1870–1956) with their decorative art and graphic works. Fuelled by this energy and inspired by Handicraft Guilds set up in Britain, the Wiener Werkstätte was established in Austria in 1903 by architect Josef Hoffman and graphic designer Koloman Moser (1868–1918). It was set up as a cooperative workshop established to bring together artists and designers in the design, manufacture and retailing of handcrafted products in the modern style. Embracing *Gesamtkunstwerk* (total work of art) and with complete artistic freedom, art and design aesthetics were unified across graphic design, textiles, fashion, ceramics, silver

Figure 1.21 This printed piece by graphic designer Leopoldine Kolbe (1870–1912) from 1907 illustrates the combination of simple, stylized florals and geometric patterning, popular with Josef Hoffman at the Wiener Werkstätte. This combination of natural forms and geometrics was also embraced as a feature of the Art Deco style. There was a significant female community at the Wiener Werkstätte and their contribution was significant; however, the male designers were often those who gained greater recognition.

and furniture. Traditional methods of production were valued and retained, resisting the pull towards mechanization happening elsewhere in industry.

Operations at the Wiener Werkstätte expanded fast as customers who could afford the goods embraced the mix of cultural references, from folk art, Arts and Crafts and patterns of the Art Nouveau aesthetic. The eclectic decorative style could be seen to anticipate the rise of ornamentation and the arrival of what was to be defined retrospectively as the Art Deco style. Sadly, the artistic vision at the workshop was threatened by commercial pressures following the First World War and the global depression in the late 1920s. The financial struggles combined with material shortages led to the closure of the workshop by

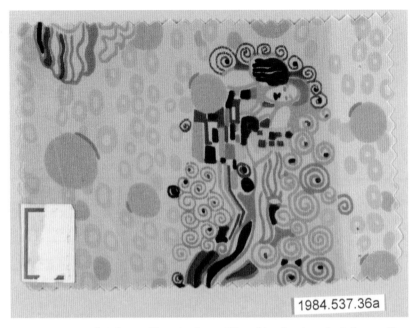

1984.537.36a

Figure 1.22 Heavily influenced by artist Gustav Klimt, this printed textile design on silk was created by Austrian-born designer Joseph Urban. The circles, swirls and embracing figures in this 1928 design clearly reference *The Kiss*, painted by Klimt in 1907/08. Urban grew up in Vienna studying architecture and followed the Wiener Werkstätte principles of unifying art and design disciplines through his life. His career in theatre design led him to America but his creative style continued to relate back to this formative period in Europe, illustrated here in a design created long after leaving Austria.

1932 but not before it had inspired design institutions such as the Bauhaus, Germany, as well as manufacturers in Paris and London.

Britain had lost the competition for the luxury market to France and was left floundering with the tail end of Art Nouveau style. As interest in modern pattern production was gaining momentum, a craft revival (echoing the Arts and Crafts ethos) offered an opportunity for consumers to invest in traditional craft techniques and handmade items. Roger Fry (1866–1934), an English painter and art critic, supporter of the Post-Impressionists and member of the Bloomsbury Group, set up the Omega Workshops in 1913, a studio of artists making products for home interiors. The aim was to build closer links between art and design practices and support his artist friends

to earn a living beyond painting. Vanessa Bell (1879–1961), Duncan Grant (1885–1978) and artists fresh from art school painted on ceramics and furniture, made rugs and designed textiles, inspired by European Fauvist and Cubist painters such as Henri Matisse (1869–1954) and Georges Braque (1882–1963). Patterns featuring abstract forms, some loosely geometric, made with brush marks and tessellating motifs jostled in unconventional pattern structures, heavily inspired by paintings on canvas. This was an antidote to the refined style of Edwardian Britain. Most items were created in workshops in London, but some textiles were screen printed in France.

Sadly, despite commissions for interior schemes and exclusive pieces, orders were limited and the press was less than supportive. Several of

Figure 1.23 *Maud* by Vanessa Bell typifies the Omega Workshops' interpretation of Post-Impressionist painting for pattern-making and surface decoration. Originally, the fabric was screen printed in France from 1913. This contemporary reissue on homeware products and interior textiles by the Charleston Trust in the UK continues to evidence the popularity and interest in the Omega Workshops.

the artists were conscientious objectors in the First World War which proved unpopular among their customer base. Lack of sales exacerbated by the war and ongoing disagreements in the group resulted in the company disbanding in 1919.

In Britain a number of designers were returning to the craft of woodblock printing to create hand-printed lengths of fabrics and wallpapers for clientele able to afford small-run craft production. In the 1920s Phyllis Barron (1890–1964) and Dorothy Larcher (1884–1952) established a dye lab and print studio to create bespoke textiles using natural dyes and resist techniques, inspired by traditional art from around the world as well as European modern art and geometric pattern construction. They showcased their designs within a gallery setting to contextualize the interior products alongside ceramics and other craft objects.

Designer Enid Marx (1902–98) learned block printing in the workshops of Barron and Larcher and was fascinated by historical artefacts and traditional pattern structures. She created printing blocks that she rotated to build larger areas of pattern, developing multiple

(b.) Alternative arrangement : printed in galled iron, with alternate lozenges printed in brown, on heavy natural cotton.

163

Figure 1.24 This pattern by Barron and Larcher echoes the jazz spirit of the Art Deco era, as well as referencing traditional Indian block printing that Larcher will have seen on her international travels. The areas of dotted and striped texture alongside solid diamonds of ink provide a lively and eye-catching zig-zag rhythm.

designs with varied visual interest from small-scale repeating motifs. She designed patterns for paper and cloth as well as authoring and illustrating children's books. She developed her traditional pattern skills in relation to modern industrial production and was one of the first women to design in an otherwise male-dominated arena, providing designs for a range of key clients, including upholstery moquette fabric for London Underground and patterns for the Curwen Press.

Modern mode 1920s–1940s

Uniting all elements of design within a building was a principle of the Bauhaus, the German avant-garde art school founded in 1919. The first director of the school, Walter Gropius (1883–1969) believed all components (lighting, furniture, textile design, etc.) contributed to the whole. Students were trained in core principles of colour, shape and form before specializing in discipline-specific workshops. Inspired by William Morris and the Arts and Crafts philosophy of well-made objects, the Bauhaus also embraced modern production methods and new materials. Modern furniture required modern fabrics, and a new generation of textile designers including Gunta Stölzl (1897–1983) and Anni Albers (1899–1994) exploited new fibres and yarns to create tactile and textural fabrics and wallcoverings for Modernist interiors that continue to inspire today's designers.

During the interwar years, particularly in Britain, there was a growing practice of manufacturers working with artists to develop designs with a Modernist aesthetic, creating woven and printed pattern for interiors of the modern home. British manufacturer William Foxton worked in this way, taking inspiration from the Wiener Werkstätte and the Bauhaus to produce innovative artist-designed textiles. Established in 1903, Foxton's company initially used block printing for textile production but by the 1920s had adopted roller printing. Foxton worked with freelance artists and designers including Minnie McLeish (1876–1957), Claud Lovat Fraser (1890–1921) and Charles Rennie Mackintosh for a fresh aesthetic away from traditional approaches in stylizing. Working as freelance designers enables individuals to work with a number of manufacturers at the same time, but it can be harder to trace the output of these designers as original artwork may be listed under the name of the manufacturer only.

Foxton was an early member of the Design and Industries Association, established with the purpose of improving the standards of British design under

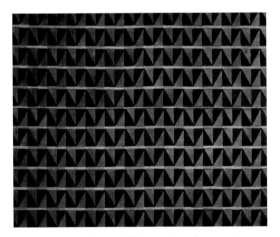

Figure 1.25 Modernist fabrics embraced geometric pattern as subject matter and this furnishing fabric by Claud Lovat Fraser for William Foxton demonstrates this with rhythmic alternate-coloured triangles and contrasting stripes.

the slogan 'Nothing Need be Ugly'. Bringing together industrialists, designers, educators and retailers, the group balanced the continuing interest in craft production with the exciting potential of mechanization in modern manufacturing.

A new Modernist architectural style developing in Europe through the first half of the twentieth century introduced concrete and steel construction methods to building schemes including the domestic home, providing opportunities to think differently in interior design. The influential Swiss-French Modernist architect Le Corbusier (1887–1965) famously wrote in 1927: 'a house is a machine for living in'. With a move away from ornate patterning and decorative features, towards clearer and open living spaces, rooms were furnished with textiles including rugs while surface designs were applied to hard surfaces such as laminates and tiles. Clean graphic pattern inspired by

Figure 1.26 Designer Hans Tisdall, born Hans Aufseeser in Germany (1910–97), spent his career predominantly designing and teaching in England, working with notable companies, including Edinburgh Weavers and Warner & Sons. This design, *Hans* from 1932, has been relaunched by Claremont Furnishing Fabrics in the original colourways: Crimson, Coffee, Marine. The dynamic directional stripes provide a rhythmic pattern relating to the visual language of jazz, popular at this time.

geometry was a natural fit, and can be seen as a development from these qualities existing in the designs of the Art Deco interiors.

Apparently lacking domestic comforts, European Modernism was considered too drastic for the Scandinavian and British markets; here, interior decoration continued to feature floral and nature-inspired patterns, colourful softened graphic printed and woven textiles and tactile accessories.

The design work of Edward Bawden (1903–1989) is often light-hearted and playful; he was a painter as well as a commercial designer for illustrations, surface design and graphic arts, fulfilling commissions for retailer Fortnum and Mason, London Underground and Penguin Books, among many others.

Innovations in synthetic dyes and fibres resulted in colourfast yarns and choice in fabrics. The industrial process of printing textiles was changing with the introduction of screen printing, albeit with interruptions from international conflicts and financial depression. Printed textiles provided a cheaper alternative to woven cloth; the screen-printing process was exciting, allowing for painterly and textured imagery to better replicate hand-drawn qualities. Manufacturers invested in screen-print production and designers embraced the technique in their work, providing a fresh look for contemporary fabrics. Designs for printed textiles continued to be hand-painted on paper before being adapted for production.

Edinburgh Weavers, an experimental wing of British manufacturer Morton Sundour, produced woven and printed fabrics that were designed by artists under the directorship of Alastair Morton (1910–63). Barbara Hepworth (1903–1975), Ben Nicholson (1894–1982) and William Scott (1913–89) were some of Morton's artist friends,

Figure 1.28 *Tree and Cow* by Edward Bawden is an interesting take on the check-pattern structure; the zig-zag field boundaries suggest an aerial view of an undulating rural landscape. The works of Bawden and his contemporary, Eric Ravilious, have enjoyed a revival of interest in the twenty-first century, resulting in these papers being relaunched by British design company, St Jude's.

Figure 1.27 Edward Bawden provides an English village narrative in this design featuring a pigeon sitting in a tree, with views through to a clock tower. This is an interesting take on the spot-pattern structure, as the pigeons and clock towers are aligned in pairs, and then placed at compass points, with four sets of pairs creating a larger circle, linking with the adjacent set of circles. This becomes noticeable when larger areas of the pattern are presented across a wall. Developed from lino block imagery, this late 1920s' wallpaper was printed lithographically on sheets rather than rolls.

transforming their ideas and visual handwriting into repeating designs to bridge the divide between fine art and textile design practices.

In Scandinavia, Modernism developed by combining the traditional love of stylized florals with the appetite for contemporary design. The European Modernists' functional approach

to hard materials in new architecture proved too harsh for the Scandinavians, who preferred comfort of pattern and soft textures in their homes. Retailer IKEA was founded in Sweden in 1943, and throughout the 1950s their product lines and sales grew, enabling consumers to furnish their homes with modern materials and products.

In printed textile design it was Austrian architect and designer Josef Frank (1885–1967) who,

Figure 1.29 This paper design for furnishing fabric by designer Dora Batty (1891–1966) illustrates a stylized folk art aesthetic, popular at this time. Batty designed *Hurstwood* for Helios in the 1940s. You can see the motifs have been altered as Batty worked, collaging new elements over the initial ideas. The flowing sprigs of foliage provide movement alongside the more static directional birds. Batty worked for other notable clients including Poole Pottery and London Transport.

on fleeing to Sweden from the Nazi threat in mainland Europe in 1934, re-established his career by creating a substantial portfolio of textile designs for interiors company Svenskt Tenn. A lifelong creative partnership was formed, despite Frank becoming exiled in America due to the Second World War. His love of pattern and nature, combined with his respect for William Morris and the pattern designs of the Arts and Crafts movement, helped him to become key in defining the Swedish aesthetic of the mid-twentieth century, still in demand today.

Post-war 1945–1960s

During and after the Second World War, rationing was in place in Britain. In 1941, the British government established the Utility Scheme providing the public with access to basic consumer goods, designed to require limited resources and simple manufacture. Enid Marx was one of the designers commissioned to produce modern and cost-effective designs for woven and printed pattern as well as laminates, featuring small-scale patterns to limit waste.

Figure 1.30 Concerned that Modernism was stark, Josef Frank wanted to create more visual interest to calm a space. Frank's patterns illustrate his fascination with the natural world, using uplifting colour and pattern in abundance. Frank explored pattern structures in order to compose the motifs within engaging rhythms or pictorial scenes such as trees and gardens, a recurring subject for him. He explored repeat rhythms by rotating the designs in order to grow new configurations. Over-printing of clean and bright colours using the screen-printing process builds to create depth of tone and saturated hues.

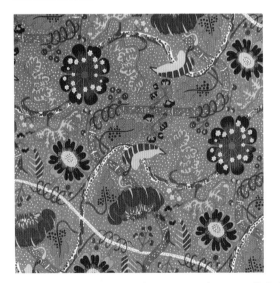

Figure 1.31a & Figure 1.31b Here two colourways of Mirakel balance the motifs quite differently, dependent on the colour, tone and size of the elements across the pattern. The darker background of (b) allows the plants to sing out from the pattern with the vine being very clear, whereas the more even-toned red colourway (a) showcases the darker dominant flower heads, rather than the vine.

Fashion designers created outfits limited by numbers of buttons, length of skirt and width of pleats, and Utility furniture was also brought to the market. This was an opportunity to convince consumers to engage with modern design of pared-back aesthetics at affordable prices during a time of austerity.

To galvanize industry and engage the public it was agreed that, in the centenary year of the Great Exhibition, there would be a new national celebration. The Festival of Britain held in 1951, attended by visitors from across the country and abroad, raised the profile of modern pattern, embracing inspiration from science and technology for the future-thinking customer. The Festival Pattern Group created numerous patterns inspired by science, including molecular structures as seen through microscopes. The British textile design industry was keen to re-establish itself through a new generation of designers

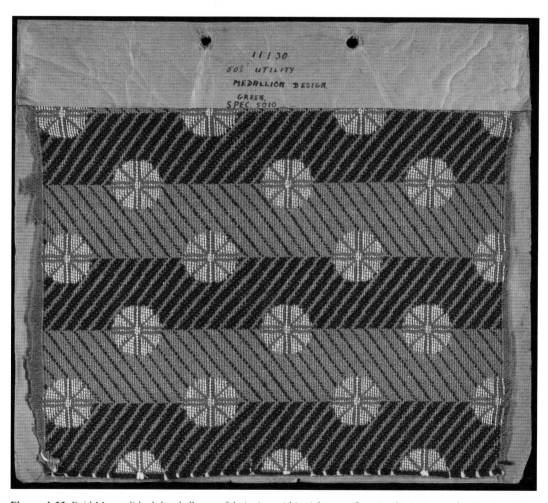

Figure 1.32 Enid Marx relished the challenge of designing within tight manufacturing limitations and enjoyed creating patterns for woven and printed textiles and laminates. The geometric design *Spot and Stripe* uses negative and positive colouring in chevrons to provide balance and visual interest to a straightforward composition of stripes and spots.

Figure 1.33 *Helmsley* by Swiss born designer Marianne Straub (1909–94) takes inspiration from the crystal structure of nylon, resulting in a diagrammatic representation of atoms. Although a woven textile, this new approach to motif generation from scientific subjects was embraced by print and weave designers alike. This design was created in 1951. Straub was considered one of the leading commercial textile designers in Britain, designing for Helios before working for Warner & Sons, a leading silk-weaving manufacturer at this time.

including Lucienne Day (1917–2010), Terence Conran (1931–2020) and émigrés from Europe, Marian Mahler (1911–83) and Jacqueline Groag (1903–86). Textiles and wallpapers offered those setting up new homes the chance to create tastes and preferences different to their parents. In industry, printed textiles were produced either by roller printing or hand screen printing, but by the end of the 1950s the mechanized process of flatbed screen printing had been adopted.

Lucienne Day's pattern designs, so evocative of this period, provided a modern abstract pattern language for the contemporary interior. Day graduated from the Royal College of Art and, after delaying her design career due to the Second World War, she established herself as a highly competent and versatile pattern designer, selling designs to manufacturers for fashion and interior textiles, including Edinburgh Weavers. Moving away from the traditional florals and inspired by painters such as Wassily Kandinsky (1866–1944) and Joan Miró (1893–1983), Day's stylized graphic patterns provided a fresh new pattern language (subsequently imitated by her competitors). As Day became braver with her abstract motifs, she gained a reputation and was soon commissioned by Heal Fabrics, a relationship she maintained for decades, designing at least six designs each year.

Robin and Lucienne Day defined post-war interiors, with Robin's modern furniture design and Lucienne's graphic aesthetic. Over several decades Lucienne collaborated with companies including Horrockses, Cole & Son, Liberty and John Lewis, but it is her significant output for Heal Fabrics that defines her legacy and continues to inspire textile designers today.

The textiles industry has always relied on freelance designers, with many well-known designers starting their careers in this way. Freelance designers are able to turn their hand to signature styles required by the commissioning company, reflecting the market of the day. Terence Conran established his reputation for contemporary design by creating abstract textile designs with a hand-drawn aesthetic for manufacturer David Whitehead Ltd during the

Figure 1.34 Lucienne Day showcased fabric and wallpaper designs at the Festival of Britain, including the award-winning *Calyx*, originally designed as furnishing fabric for her husband, industrial designer Robin Day (1915–2010), in order to coordinate with the contemporary furniture he was exhibiting. The cup-shaped motifs and linear details suggest floral forms, but equally appear as kites rising in the air. The use of dashed lines lightens the visual weight as does the textural areas of some of the cup forms.

1950s, including *Chequers*, showcased at the Festival of Britain. Conran's vision that good design should be for all, rather than the few, was realized in the opening of the first Habitat retail store in London during 1964 where he made contemporary design accessible to the British public. The store showcased textiles alongside furniture and accessories styled as room interiors to give guidance and inspiration to the general public.

It is not uncommon for freelance designers, often women, to sell artwork to a number of different clients without being acknowledged as originator at the point of public sale; consequently, tracing designers can be very difficult retrospectively. Sheila Bownas (1925–2007) is one such name we are now aware of since her archive was picked up at auction following her death. Bownas was a freelance designer predominantly through the 1950s to 1970s, selling to

Figure 1.35 *Spectators* (1953), one of Lucienne Day's favourites, playfully features bespectacled onlookers forming wide horizontal stripes, balancing the linear vertical stripes of the characters. Day's use of red alongside black and white strikingly and expertly exploits negative and positive shapes in a cost-effective way.

Figure 1.36 This unsold design by Sheila Bownas for the children's market is playful and reminiscent of book illustrations of the era. There is movement in the dancing children, our eyes moving from one group to the other. The use of blue and red clothing creates energy and contrast upon the yellow background.

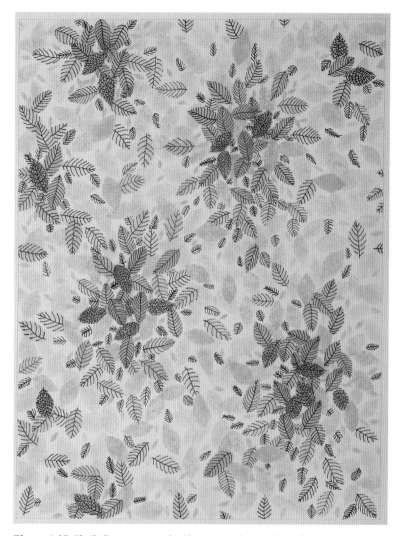

Figure 1.37 Sheila Bownas created wide-ranging designs that reflect the stylistic features of the decades she worked through: conversational prints, geometrics, large-scale graphic patterns, mark making and floral designs. The visual depth in this pattern is provided by the tonal variations of the printed leaf shapes and united as areas of focus by the black linear details creating clusters of visual interest. Hand-drawn graphic patterns were commonly applied to hard surfaces such as kitchen laminates and vinyl furniture upholstery.

companies including Liberty, Crown Wallpapers and Marks and Spencer.

Since its commercial uptake for printing textiles in the 1930s, screen printing continued to evolve; by the 1950s it was possible to print photographic images by screen, enabling designers to think in new ways to create images away from drawing, painting and traditional printmaking. Hungarian émigré to Britain Tibor Reich (1916–96) was one such designer. Alongside a significant output of woven fabrics for notable commissions including Concorde,

Figure 1.38 Tibor Reich's new photographic pattern process, *Fotextur*, developed in the mid-1950s, the subject of a British Pathé News film in 1957, involved cutting up photographs of textures found in nature and repositioning them as new compositions for repeat patterns using tessellating shapes. Using this new process, areas of monotone textures from tree bark, leaves and rocks were used to create imagery for furnishing fabrics.

Figure 1.39 Here you can see Tibor Reich cutting and testing compositions from the photographs of nature, to make patterns for screen printing.

the QE2 cruise liner, 10 Downing Street and the royal household, his photographic design approach *Fotextur* was developed for screen-printed textiles.

Upbeat escapism and calm retreats, late 1960s–1980s

Bright colours, bold motifs and playful patterns shaped the look of interiors in the 1960s. The combination of synthetic fibres and dyes being developed along with the influence of popular culture established upbeat energy in designs of the period. In London, the fashion scene led the way in creating new codes of mixing and matching pattern and fabrics; the interiors market

subsequently embraced this energy, creating new takes on historic patterns, but bigger and much brighter.

A new generation of designers developed their handwriting and design interests during post-war training at art schools where experimentation and vision for how art and design could shape the modern world liberated them from previous design conventions. Althea McNish (1924–2020) was a leading influence on pattern design, bringing a colourful spirit of optimism to post-war British consumers. Already an established artist, she arrived in Britain from Trinidad and Tobago in the 1950s and studied textile design at the Royal College of Art, immediately gaining high-profile clients (including Liberty and Heal Fabrics) for her flamboyant and colourful patterns.

Figure 1.40 This screen-printed textile design, *Flamingo* by Tibor Reich, uses his *Fotextur* process to dramatic effect, employing broad vertical stripes to add visual weight to the texture in the photographs.

Figure 1.41 Australian-born international designer Florence Broadhurst (1899–1977) took inspiration from her adventurous travels to feed her exuberant design work. Her patterns are full of the energy and glamour reminiscent of the Art Deco period. This design – *Japanese Floral* – suggests inspiration from her travels to the Orient. The multi-directional flower heads on stems provide a playful spirit of movement and dance. © 2022 Florence Broadhurst. All rights reserved.

Figure 1.42 In this reissued wallpaper design *Egrets* by Florence Broadhurst the egrets provide character to the pattern, standing proud amongst the branches and flowers. The eye-catching, attractive fan shape of the wings in the bird facing to the right, contrasting with the upright egret looking left, provides a striking combination and opens the design up to take the eye across the walls. Note also that the colour of the branches of the tree are the same as the flowers and birds, resulting in a unified rhythm from all the elements. © 2022 Florence Broadhurst. All rights reserved.

Marimekko, a Finnish lifestyle brand launched in 1951, established itself on the world design stage with bold prints for fashion and interiors through the 1960s, cheerfully providing colour and pattern in homes across the world. With a reputation for bold stripes and very large-scale repeating colourful prints featuring stylized graphic florals, the brand has continued to evolve and sustain a loyal customer base. Marimekko's most iconic pattern, *Unikko*, a large-scale floral motif, heavily stylized and not for the shy, was designed by Maija Isola (1927–2001) in 1964, summing up the playful aesthetic of the time when it was designed and remaining popular today.

Despite the excitement of the faster and more furious pace of post-war Britain with a growing consumer market driven by fashion and popular culture, and interior schemes featuring attention-seeking wallpapers and colourful fabrics,

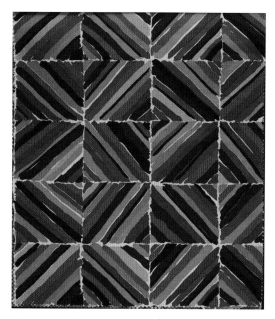

Figure 1.44 The signature style of Collier Campbell patterns, upbeat hand-painted marks, are captured here in screen-printed design *Kasak* for Liberty. The loose geometric pattern designed in 1973 originally for fashion fabric and later for furnishing fabric, features diagonal stripes in tonal hues constructed in soft squares, providing an undulating grid.

Figure 1.43 In this design relaunched in the twenty-first century, *Papyrus* by Florence Broadhurst, the natural forms of bullrushes and papyrus flow across the design creating depth, as if looking through the plants on the riverbank of the Nile in Egypt. The bullrushes provide formal stripes for the papyrus to twist among, crossing the uprights with a diagonal rhythm. The colourways in this image utilize tones of coral, greens and blues, providing harmony and sophistication.

there remained a more conservative interest in pattern language which continues to be a significant feature in the European market. In the 1970s a romantic Victorian revival renewed interest in Arts and Crafts, taking inspiration from William Morris and his peers, providing a nostalgic embrace of nature for the calm and restful domestic interior.

Market stalwarts Sandersons and G.P & J Baker have extensive archives in which to develop designs and reissue classic patterns in new colourways appropriate to contemporary customer tastes. Both Arts and Crafts and Art Nouveau-inspired patterns were recoloured and reissued at this time. Traditional pattern structures in printed pastel and muted tones sat alongside sprigs, spots and stripes of a more relaxed and contemporary interpretation of the historical references of the mid-nineteenth century.

The second half of the twentieth century saw a number of interiors brands establishing their place in the British home as well as the international export market. Osborne and Little joined the market in the 1960s and balanced the need to provide both classic and contemporary styles in interior textiles (including woven and printed fabrics as well as trims). Designers Guild, a luxury interiors brand established by Tricia

Figure 1.45 The 1980s saw an increase in foreign travel to sunny locations, and when Collier Campbell were too busy working to fit in a holiday, they designed a pattern collection for furnishing fabric to provide the holiday feeling, including the iconic pattern *Cote d'Azur* for Christian Fischbacher in 1983. Printed on cotton, the design features stylized plants, balconies, awnings and birds in flight, paying homage to painters such as Henri Matisse, Raoul Dufy and Sonia Delaunay. The striking signature hand-painted marks and exquisite colour palette generously play with the repeating motifs, resulting in an eye-catching, rhythmic pattern. The design was adapted in 1991 for bedlinen, licensed in the United States and Europe. You can read more about Sarah Campbell's career in Chapter 3.

Guild in 1970, offered sumptuous colourful and textured fabrics, including some collections with Indian influence inspired by block-printed formal pattern structures on fabrics and home accessories. Laura Ashley, a brand renowned for small-scale repeating prints for fashion and interiors, provided a romantic rural spirit, even launching a pattern featuring a geometric lattice print, *Mr Jones*, in 1984, in honour of the Gothic Revivalist Owen Jones.

Liberty continued to provide customers with patterns for fashion and interiors inspired by their extensive archive, enjoying a renewed interest in the Art Nouveau style that had established the brand identity back in 1875. Liberty have also continued to look forwards, working with contemporary designers to launch new pattern collections (and build the archive). Sisters Susan Collier and Sarah Campbell (Collier Campbell) created a number of designs for Liberty, capturing the public's eagerness to embrace pattern and colour once again.

Encouraged by television programmes introducing accessible interior design advice and DIY ideas, consumers embraced home decoration in the 1980s. European audiences were encouraged to be brave, transforming rooms with brighter paint colours and striking graphic wallpapers alongside contemporary furniture and home products. Terence Conran's Habitat was perfectly placed to sell to the UK domestic homewares market, providing much-needed and welcome change from the beige colour palette of yesteryear. IKEA, the Swedish retailer of furniture and home accessories, had been opening stores, initially in Scandinavia, spreading across Europe in the 1970s, and by the 1980s stores were open in the United States and UK. Modernist design, new materials and colourful patterned textiles were accessible to millions of consumers, keen to embrace the future of home interiors.

Postmodern magic and digital design 1980s–2020s

The neoclassical revival in the nineteenth century was based on truth, on judgements of right and wrong decided upon centuries before in ancient classical civilization. These rules continue to guide pattern design, with traditional pattern structures such as the stripe, spot, ogee and trellis utilized with a certain sense of reliability and expectation throughout the last two centuries of design.

Patterns are designed to repeat across a wallpaper or fabric, mainly due to methods of production, and designers are used to fulfilling that brief. Postmodernism challenged this expectation. What was known about pattern and surface design for interiors—concepts, image-making and production methods—was ripped up and reconstructed, enabled by a return

Figure 1.46a & b Since the 1980s, Timney Fowler have embraced classical imagery to create many wallpaper and fabric designs featuring columns, carved statues and friezes. In a striking monochrome palette, *Roman Heads* references engraved illustrations for studying classical architecture, and yet deconstructs classical motifs for the postmodern interior. The design has been available as wallpaper, fabrics and ceramics since its launch.

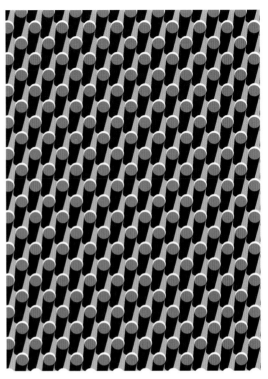

Figure 1.47 Design duo Eley Kishimoto have spent more than two decades exploring and testing pattern construction in relation to both fashion and interior contexts. With a strong graphic visual identity and presence, and a close eye on quality design and execution, their patterns have featured on fashion collections, wallpapers, furnishing products, galleries and more. Disassociating themselves from trends and passing phases, the designers embrace each challenge by creating bespoke pattern solutions for the global market. This pattern contains visual movement; the eye is encouraged to follow the flow of graphic motifs, almost reminiscent of fur but equally conveying a three-dimensional world beyond the pattern through a feeling of never-ending depth.

Figure 1.48 *Sun Loving Bollards* by Eley Kishimoto utilizes the traditional spot pattern motif while referencing street furniture. The shadows in black provide a sense of depth in the pattern.

to craft production by some, and an embrace of digital production by others.

The subject matter considered appropriate and acceptable for domestic interiors has been updated considerably, bringing imagery of fast food, make-up and cosmetics, fake bricks and much more, into our homes. Classical

heads floating across the wallpaper by Timney Fowler and street bollards by Eley Kishimoto are good examples of alternative approaches with motifs in pattern taking on the postmodern approach.

At the start of the twenty-first century, a new breed of designers was challenging the conventional application of wallpaper within interior spaces, from retail environments, private clubs and domestic dwellings. Rather than providing 10-metre rolls of repeating pattern, designers played with notions of bespoke, unique and handcrafted, embracing old and new technologies, and reinventing the predictable roll of printed pattern. Tracy Kendall offers wallpaper

Figure 1.49 In Deborah Bowness's postgraduate collection *Hooks and Frocks* at the Royal College of Art in 1999, the non-repeating wallpapers feature full-size printed items of furniture and clothing alongside physical items, exploring the *trompe-l'œil* tradition of surface design for interiors while presenting non-repeating wall-based decoration. Monochromatic photographic images are printed, and blocks of colours are then hand screen printed on to the wallpaper lengths, challenging the expectation of how to hang wallpapers. You can read more about Deborah Bowness's career in Chapter 3.

Figure 1.50 A 10-metre roll of wallpaper from Kirath Ghundoo's *Mix 'n' Match* collection enables customers to decide how to compose the pattern across the walls, taking the design process through to the installation stage. Digitally printed, featuring a range of repeating motifs and graphic pattern, the wallpaper has been designed to create numerous iterations of design.

featuring buttons, sequins and oversized printed cutlery, while Rachel Kelly screen prints individual lengths of floral motifs, providing laser-cut stickers for customers to add. The 10-metre roll was no longer expected to contain fully repeating designs, with designers including Deborah Bowness and Kirath Ghundoo enabling customers to hang the wallpaper in a way to suit their own interior space.

In the computer age it is possible to generate artwork without picking up a pencil or paint brush. Digital imagery constructed of pixels in highly saturated, multicolour files is now possible;

a far cry from the colour-separated artwork of the woodblock and flatbed screen print. Postmodern pattern design has questioned and challenged the convention of formal pattern structures, embracing new opportunities for compositions. Computer software can generate print-ready repeating tiles from artwork and even has the capability to generate random, neverending patterns. For some designers, getting rid of the need for pattern repeat as a means of reproduction in the manufacturing process opens up a new set of opportunities in pattern making.

Figure 1.51 Daniel Heath creates screen-printed designs for wallpaper and other surface materials, embracing the flexibility that craft production offers. *Onyx Skyline* is reminiscent of the Art Deco period, with luxurious metallic finishes and formally arranged geometric details, including the arching starburst motif.

Designers have challenged conventional ideas of products for walls, sofas, windows and floors. Bespoke production, both digital and handmade, has been embraced by designers wanting to provide an alternative relationship with the home, allowing them to offer unique design solutions.

Designers continue to test their creative ideas alongside and up against traditional rules and expectations, preserving handcraft processes and embracing technological advances. When we understand what has gone before us in design, how previous creatives played their part, we are able to respond and innovate in order to continue this fascinating journey of pattern design in our homes and world around us.

2

The Basics—Making Patterns

Introduction

This chapter introduces and explains the various considerations a designer makes when creating repeating patterns for interior contexts, either for domestic home furnishings or the contract market, such as hospitality, office or educational settings. This is not a step-by-step guide as there are many different ways to design patterns, but with an understanding of this chapter, designers can employ components wisely, building strong repeating patterns however they create artwork.

Examples in this chapter include design development and patterns by outstanding contemporary designers with differing experience and working methods, highlighting the multiple approaches to pattern building. All

have something worth sharing, enabling others to understand options for their own practice, in traditional or digital methods.

Sections of this chapter explain various elements through the design journey, coming together to influence decisions throughout the process. Some designers work with black and white motifs and apply colour later, others are directed by colour from the start. There are designers who create highly successful designs without picking up a pencil, using digital methods throughout. Others rely on processes such as lino printing or painting to define the aesthetic of the motifs, only digitizing at the later stages ready for production. There are many ways to create pattern, and this chapter aims to highlight some common working methods.

Figure 2.1 *Biophillia* by Kit Miles has been created by combining hand-drawing and digital manipulation.

Figure 2.2 Keeping a sketchbook for motifs is a good way to test and develop pattern ideas. Sketchbook by Molly Jean Brown.

Pattern language and process

There are many words used in design to help describe qualities and technical aspects of the pattern process and outcomes. This section defines these words and explores them within the process of designing, to better inform decisions made when designing pattern.

Motifs are the elements that come together to make a **pattern**; they are the separate details within the design. **Composition** refers to how those motifs are arranged. Whether it repeats or not, the resulting pattern can utilize different **pattern structures** (e.g. **stripe**, **trellis** or **spot**) in its composition.

Compositions can have varying **rhythms**. Think about listening to a piece of music and how the sounds of the instruments vary but contribute to the complete sound; the notes from different instruments provide different qualities and accents in the differing rhythms and phrases. A pattern can explore and enhance visual rhythmic qualities through colour, scale, texture and proportion. Patterns can be regular and uniform if the motifs are organized, or scattered if they are loosely and unevenly arranged. Some compositions are busy, or cluttered, others more open with larger spacing (**negative space**) between the motifs. A **repeat** is the design area containing motifs that is duplicated across the surface.

Key themes in pattern design include **florals** and **geometrics**, **abstracts** and **conversational** designs but within these themes are other categories such as **international**, **camouflage**, **animal** and **micro**. Defining subject matter, how artwork is created, and **stylizing** the motifs establishes personal design style.

motif — *the elements that join together to make a* **pattern;**

composition — *the layout of motifs in a pattern;*

pattern structure — *a formal composition, often based on traditional designs such as stripe, check or trellis;*

rhythm — *the visual effect of the combined design elements;*

negative space — *the areas around the motifs within a design, often the background, just as vital to consider;*

repeat — *the area of artwork that will be duplicated in production to create lengths of fabric or wallpaper, for example;*

stylizing — *drawing in a style that maintains an element recognizable but altered; a visual interpretation of something.*

DESIGN THEMES

florals — *designs featuring plants and flowers, a key theme for textile design in interiors and fashion contexts;*

geometric — *motifs based on geometric shapes (circles, squares, triangles), often tessellating or intersecting;*

abstract — *a pattern that does not stem from a physical theme; sometimes the term abstract is used if a motif has been heavily stylized;*

conversational — *a design featuring small scenes, characters or objects; a* **conversational** *design suggests a narrative between the motifs—see* **toile;**

international — *references linked to global cultures and heritage processes;*

camouflage — *traditional military pattern, often with a contemporary twist, more usual in fashion prints;*

animal — *designs referencing animal fur and skin;*

micro — *very small motifs with a small repeating tile;*

toile — *(from the French term,* toile de Jouy*) featuring a narrative in small scenes, usually printed in one colour on a pale base cloth, picturing pastoral scenes as well as commemorative events.*

Figure 2.3 This floral pattern by Hannah Whitehouse features detailed hand–drawn flowers with silhouettes that add depth to the design. The negative space around the motifs provides important breathing space.

Figure 2.4 Tamasyn Gambell's *Trigonometry* pattern is a geometric design, utilizing triangles as the single unit motif connected through the use of negative and positive shapes to form larger-shaped colour blocks of triangles, squares and parallelograms. The striped diamonds printed over the top of the yellow and grey shapes provide a discreet yet formal alternating chequerboard.

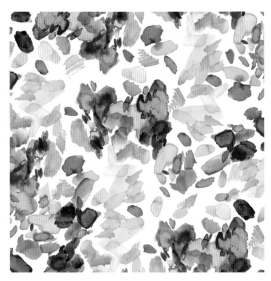

Figure 2.6 This abstract design by Bluebellgray is made by hand-painting and drawing to create a scattered pattern, also referred to as an all-over design. The structure is informal, with different areas of visual interest, picked out with accents of bright pinks within the blue / green palette. The different directions of the brushed marks provide a multi-directional rhythm.

Figure 2.5 *Ona*, by Eva Sonaike, is a formal arrangement of a spot pattern structure, referencing traditional African pattern aesthetic. The individual bold motifs sit in offset rows on a ground consisting of a micro pattern, a very small-scale detailed pattern providing a visual texture to hold the larger motifs.

Designing pattern is like making a meal—the better the ingredients, the stronger the final design will be; it is difficult to add quality later. The quality of the line, the shapes and level of detail need to be considered from the beginning, ensuring the very best motifs are present throughout the design process.

There are many traditional pattern structures that designers find useful to engage with. These structures provide a scaffolding to place motifs in relation to other elements in the design. Within a design collection it is common to include a variety of pattern structures, providing different visual rhythms. Making decisions early on about the style of the motifs and design composition can focus the designer's mind; with greater efficiency more designs can be created in the time available. The pattern structure exists within the repeating design tile and does not necessarily define how a pattern will be repeated.

Figure 2.7 *Hayfield*, by Marthe Armitage, is a busy block-printed pattern with visual texture provided by the stylized plants and tonal areas. Despite being a one-colour design, there are many plant details to notice, keeping the eye moving through the design. The darker dense areas of thistle leaves can be used to identify the repeat within the pattern.

Figure 2.8 This initial idea for a repeating pattern by Florence Poppy Dennis uses supermarket aisles as horizontal stripes to structure a conversational design of dogs shopping.

Figure 2.9 Design duo Timorous Beasties brought the *toile de Jouy* to a modern audience with the launch of a series of city-inspired designs as a contemporary take on the pattern traditionally associated with pastoral scenes. Here, landmarks of Edinburgh, local scenes and public transport provide a backdrop for people busy in the city. You can read an interview with Timorous Beasties in Chapter 3.

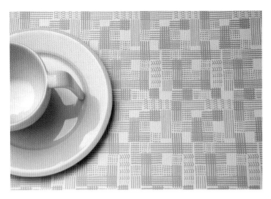

Figure 2.10 This micro pattern by Kate Farley is printed on laminate for tabletops, and provides small-scale visual noise, contrasting with larger-scale patterns in the same interior scheme.

SOME KEY PATTERN STRUCTURES

check — *evenly spaced intersecting horizontal and vertical lines or filled squares creating a square grid design, usually with one or two colours;*

damask — *reversible woven patterned cloth, inspiring printed pattern of symmetrical / mirrored elaborate scrolls and foliage;*

diamond — *a repeating pattern of contrasting diamonds or elongated squares, also known as* **harlequin**;

diaper — *a term taken from woven cloth, small uniform geometric design of interlocking shapes such as diamonds, rectangles or squares;*

dogtooth check — *two-tone tessellating checks that each have four points breaking out of the sides, traditionally a woven pattern;*

lattice — *an open framework of diagonal lines crossing; see* **trellis**;

ogee — *a continuous double-curved S-shaped line or solid hourglass form, usually on a vertical drop;*

paisley — *referring to the motif of the teardrop (buta) shape, rather than an overall design;*

plaid — *criss-crossing lines with two or more colours, of varying sizes and colours, crossing at right angles;*

polka dot — *solid circles of the same size in a uniform arrangement, often on the diagonal grid;*

spot — *motifs closely grouped, appearing as if scattered, but in a set grid of rows / columns, maybe referred to as a sateen repeat;*

stripe — *a design of vertical or horizontal lines;*

trellis — *an open framework of diagonal lines intersecting, often as a support for more flowing motifs over the top (see* **lattice**).

Formal pattern structures often reference periods in history and reoccur from time to time, but can also reference cultural and geographical belonging, so this can be useful to explore in relation to a brief. Strong structures such as a traditional woven **damask** pattern or **paisley** motifs from Asia have been reinterpreted in printed textiles over the centuries and still find their way into contemporary design collections. Designers need to ensure they are making the appropriate cultural and historical reference rather than cause offence with simplistic imitation. Designs from the Arts and Crafts era are very different structurally from Pop Art patterns of the 1960s, so it is important to understand the distinctive features of design work in each period and how they meet the design brief or trend inspiration being followed. Once the principles of specific pattern structures are understood they can be adapted and variations explored, mixing up the features of each for exciting results—for example, using a trellis with trailing plants over the top, or mixing an ogee with a strong stripe.

Figure 2.11 In *Paisley Crescent*, Mini Moderns have created a contemporary interpretation of the traditional paisley pattern, providing a clean graphic design in vibrant tangerine. Working on a computer, it is important to test the scale of motifs throughout the design process as it can be hard to relate to the scale of the final intended product at a screen. The larger individual *buta* motifs in this design could fill a computer screen.

Figure 2.12 Stripes are a staple in an interiors collection, most commonly vertical stripes, but horizontal stripes are also on the market. These stripe patterns in Eva Sonaike's *Falomo* interiors collection contain rhythmic textural elements.

Figure 2.13 An informal stripe design can be made from motifs arranged formally in vertical columns or horizontal rows. This can add interest to the stripe and provide a different voice in the collection of patterns. This pattern by Tasha Warren has contrasting flower heads and foliage growing up an informal stripe structure.

It is usual for designers to create collections of patterns that work together across an interior scheme and on different surfaces or products. A collection may have any number of patterns, often between six and ten designs, with one or two designs considered the **main / feature designs** that include a greater number of motifs or offer more flamboyance as the signature voice of the collection. Other designs in the collection, referred to as **coordinates**, play a supporting role and tend to be smaller in scale, and less complex. Designs in the collection will vary in their use of scale and colour to provide visual contrasts across the overall collection. A range of pattern structures will also be used, helping to provide breadth of design outcomes.

There are terms that define design layouts that are likely to feature within a collection relating to pattern, structure and composition. If a pattern of motifs flows evenly across the composition it may be referred to as an **all-over** design. If the motifs face one way a design is known as **directional**, while if the motifs are facing multiple directions, it is **multi-directional** (perfect

Photography by Harry Crowder, Styled by Home and Found

Figure 2.14 This trellis pattern, *Dashwood* by Hamilton Weston, appears to be simple but includes highly considered elements. The pale diagonal lines create the trellis structure containing individual floral motifs. Intertwined with the pale trellis are dotted wavy lines creating rounded squares. Where the trellis lines meet the wavy lines, dotted circles provide a fastening device, holding the delicate structure in place.

Figure 2.15 Interlocking circles provide the formal geometric structure in this wallpaper design, *Hanbury* by Kate Farley. The circular motifs are constructed using a range of positive and negative elements providing visual interest through the textures and details of linocuts. You can read more about the design process of Hanbury in the section: The making of Hanbury (Introduction).

Figure 2.17 This interpretation of an ogee pattern, *Ijoba*, by Eva Sonaike, relies on the towering up of circles to provide the negative and positive S-shapes associated with the ogee structure. The decoration within the circles provides a three-dimensionality, contrasting with the background texture.

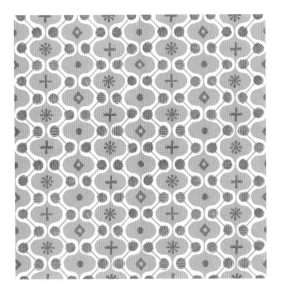

Figure 2.16 Kate Farley demonstrates the ogee structure of narrowing and widening S-curved forms here. The negative and positive shapes provide depth in the design and the darker small motifs add visual interest.

for upholstery as the pattern can flow over the different faces of the furniture and still look the right way up). A **scattered** design would feature isolated motifs distributed across the design. A **turnover** includes symmetrical elements where the motif or design has been mirrored. A **placement** design, sometimes referred to as an **engineered** print, does not repeat but is a self-contained design appropriate for a specific place on an item—for example, on a scarf, the front of a T-shirt or the face of a cushion. It is also possible to combine these layouts—for example, a directional spot pattern.

Figure 2.18 This pattern collection, *Lilaea*, designed by Clarissa Hulse for Harlequin, demonstrates how designs can work together to define an interiors scheme. Each pattern carries out a different job, such as providing drama or calm, alongside the other patterns and surfaces. Here the curtains provide statement elements of grasses in dramatic broad horizontal stripes of colour. Cushions are often used to add accent colours from the palette, where a hue may be too dominant for large surface areas.

COLLECTION PATTERN TERMS

main / feature designs — *the designs that are key to the collection, often most complex and collection defining, carrying the strongest identity;*

coordinates — *supporting designs in a collection, showing a resemblance to the main designs;*

all-over — *a pattern that spreads across the surface, less formally than a stripe or check;*

directional — *a design that has a clear right way up (e.g. horses standing in a field);*

multi-directional — *a design that can be read from several directions, with no particular 'right way up';*

scattered — *sometimes referred to as a **tossed**, or **spot**, design;*

turnover — *the pattern is flipped horizontally or vertically to extend the design, also **mirrored**;*

placement — *a design / motif placed singularly on a specific part of a product, and which therefore does not repeat; sometimes referred to as an **engineered** pattern.*

Figure 2.19 This directional pattern by Ed Kluz for St Jude's features motifs that have a right way up. The striking use of triangles and parallelograms in contrasting colours and textures adds visual texture and rhythm alongside the static, directional elements.

Figure 2.20 The thunder clouds in Abigail Edwards' wallpaper pattern *Storm Clouds* are scattered across the brooding skies, connected by flashes of lightning in a downward direction, providing informal diagonal shapes as visual interest and movement. Wallpapers are often directional in their design.

A freelance designer may create collections of designs for their **portfolio** to show a number of **clients** but if any of the designs are sold from one collection, the remaining designs in the collection must not share any motifs with the sold designs as this compromises **intellectual property**. Once a design is sold, the artwork including all the motifs belong to the client, and they would not want to see the same motifs elsewhere on

the market. To avoid this happening, it is wise to create plenty of motifs for each collection, so no two designs share elements, even when they look like they belong together as a collection of designs. Any unsold designs can be reworked to create difference before showing a new client. If

Figure 2.21 These three geometric designs from Kate Farley's *Plot to Plate* collection each provide a different rhythm. The left-hand design, *VVV*, is a stripe including groups of V-motifs rising diagonally. The centre design, *XO*, is a spot, with each motif loosely placed on a grid. The crosses inside the spot motif provide diagonal rhythm. The blue design, *XXVV*, on the right is an all-over design. A grid of small rectangular tiles provides horizontal and vertical stripes. It has the smallest repeat tile of the three designs.

a brand generates and takes a whole collection to market, some motifs can be used across the collection (likewise for own brand collections).

Researching artists and designers can provide inspiration to try something new. It helps to be aware of ways designers have previously arranged motifs to create patterns, but motifs should never be copied from other designers.

portfolio — *a collection of artwork and designs showcasing a designer's potential, through previous projects;*

clients — *those who commission designs and buy artwork, including design studios, manufacturers or retailers;*

intellectual property — *ownership of artwork and designs.*

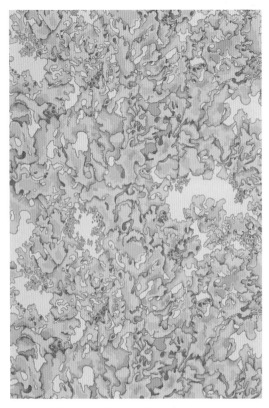

Figure 2.22a This organic, all-over pattern, *Lichen* by Abigail Edwards, in a soft, painterly style provides a tranquil spirit.

Figure 2.22b Here Abigail Edwards' *Lichen* can be seen in an interior context. Designers must think a few steps ahead to anticipate the overall effect of a design across a large surface area, likely to be considerably larger than the sampling artwork size.

Figure 2.23 Placement prints by Timorous Beasties being flatbed screen printed by hand, ready for cushion covers.

Choosing the look, making motifs

There are general questions to consider when starting to design. What will the pattern look like? Does the brief ask for something specific? Some designers follow **trends** to guide design identity, ensuring relevance to contemporary looks in specific contexts such as fashion, interiors and the automotive industry. Trends are compiled and published by forecasters communicating key concepts, colour and material directions relating to particular seasons and

Figure 2.24 Without having to consider pattern structures or how a design will repeat, initial drawings can be experimental and expressive. Molly Brown established the look of a collection by making bright drawings and collages to explore the qualities she had in mind.

global issues. WGSN and Colour Hive are two leading trend companies who sell trend intelligence and design directions to guide the design industry.

Some designers work intuitively, taking many hours to evolve the **visual language** of a design to make decisions, while others work faster and more directly, with a very clear idea of what the **client brief** requires. Each designer's creative process can vary considerably from that of their peers, and as a result of who they are employed by or whether they are running their own business. Processes such as drawing, collage, painting, printmaking and photography are commonly used to generate pattern artwork,

as well as digital drawing with a graphic tablet and computer image manipulation. Whichever way the artwork is generated, it is vital to design what the client asks for, at an appropriate cost, to agreed deadlines.

What is the style, or **aesthetic**, of the pattern? Creating a **mood board** of visual research provides a designer with key directions that will be unique and appropriate. The mood board should be kept to hand and referred back to as a design evolves. Creating ideas from a range of rich sources provides originality. Reliance on secondary references from other designers should be avoided, as this can make an artwork feel derivative.

trends — *formalized forecasts of future design directions, including colour, concepts, materials and applications;*

visual language — *the message being communicated in the design through the style or aesthetic of elements;*

client brief — *the project set by the client for the designer to complete;*

aesthetic — *the way something looks, often referred to as the beauty of something;*

mood board — *a physical or digital board that provides an outline of design inspiration to guide a project, including customer profile, themes, pattern language, colour palette.*

A brief may ask for flowers and birds in a playful, whimsical style: what flowers and birds would be appropriate? should they be native to a particular part of the world, such as rainforest species, or English country gardens' flora and fauna? A loose, dreamy style with a slightly cheeky spirit

Figure 2.25 Trend companies provide the designer with visual references and design direction relating to particular concepts linked to international research and social developments. Here Colour Hive present images for Kinship for SS20.

Figure 2.26 Clarissa Hulse's designs have a distinctive look, featuring silhouettes of plant stems and other botanical forms generated from photographs and drawings. These are edited via design software before being exposed on to the silkscreen. Hulse designs through the process of screen printing, sampling artwork by layering the imagery at the print table to form satisfying visual rhythms and engaging colour combinations.

to the birds, so they appear light-hearted, could meet the brief. Inks and watercolour paints, with loose pencil work or fine liner pen for details, may be appropriate.

Watery, inky, **fluid** shapes suggesting flowers can create an informal relaxed look, while a drawing of flowers with straight lines along a ruler, cut-out paper shapes or digitally generated imagery may look more **graphic** in style. How the artwork is created plays a significant role in whether the end result is appropriate for the brief. A designer's portfolio style may be the reason they have been commissioned but this must be clarified from the start. In some instances, a client will be happy to see initial ideas so that the right look for the design is achieved before too much time is committed.

fluid — *the pattern visually flows from one motif to another, suggesting movement;*
graphic — *usually referring to bold, clean and diagrammatic printed imagery.*

Motifs should be explored and tested, working with the ingredients in varying combinations to see what looks interesting. Is there enough motif variation, colour, scale, visual texture to give interest to the overall pattern? You can incorporate photographic imagery and explore digital manipulation techniques alongside hand processes.

To help a pattern **flow**, more ingredients can be added, but motifs should relate to each other, offering visual interest and a satisfying composition. Time should be taken to experiment as motifs can behave differently when

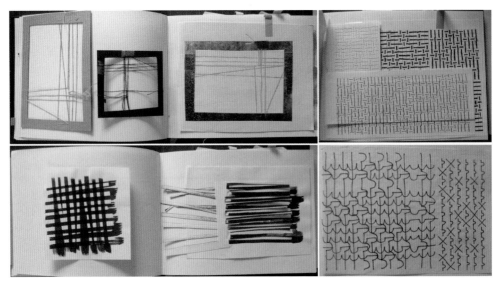

Figure 2.27 Testing plenty of ideas out to determine the visual language of a pattern is really important. Be experimental and think about the qualities that are appropriate to the brief. The *Construct* collection by Kate Farley is inspired by woven fabrics, so drawing was used to explore the idea of yarns crossing over and under one another, as the warp and weft threads do on the loom.

Figure 2.28 Experimenting with colour and mark making can help ensure the style of the pattern can be carried through the design process. Here Fiona, founder of Bluebellgray, tests the palette with motifs in watercolours.

Figure 2.29 The movement in this conversational print, *High-Wire* by Daniel Heath, is highly appropriate for the subject matter. There is energy in the individually drawn motifs as well as their relationship to neighbouring motifs, providing a narrative of circus energy and rhythmic elements across the design.

Figure 2.30 This playful pattern, *Madame Ziggle* by Ottoline, suggests a jazz rhythm in the vertical zig-zag and wavy lines; the accompanying dots add to the frivolous mood. The wallpaper would need to be considerably altered if the client required a design with a serious mood.

placed alongside other motifs. Each motif has a job: leading the eye, creating links, calming, or adding excitement to the overall **visual statement**. The motifs are important but so are the negative spaces. Are there awkward areas that need more work?—for example, does a flower stem appear cut off abruptly, or a flying bird look cramped? When a design is put into repeat, the overall effect can alter considerably, and elements may need adjusting again.

flow — *the fluidity of the design elements, whether they feel connected or disjointed;*

visual statement — *the particular look of the artwork,* **the visual language** *or* **aesthetic.**

Drawings can be made as single motifs as well as clusters, to test how elements of the design can work together, to generate variety and visual interest from the beginning. Drawing from life can be an excellent way to get to know a subject, making lots of different studies to create exciting and dynamic motifs. It can be more difficult to make engaging drawings from photographs and digital screens as the subject is already flat.

Figure 2.31 Testing motifs alongside others enables exploration of relationships and dynamics between the elements to be contained within the pattern. Tasha Warren has painted and cut out collaged elements to physically design the pattern. Motifs will then be photographed as a record before being scanned in and digitally arranged for the printing of the design on to wallpaper and fabric.

Figure 2.32 These sketchbook pages illustrate how Molly Jean Brown has tested initial ideas in coloured pencil to capture the essence of the design concept, before exploring through collage flat-colour shapes and motifs. Designs can evolve each time they are redrawn, so it is good to spend time playing with the motifs using different processes, and learning what works, before deciding on the final look of the artwork.

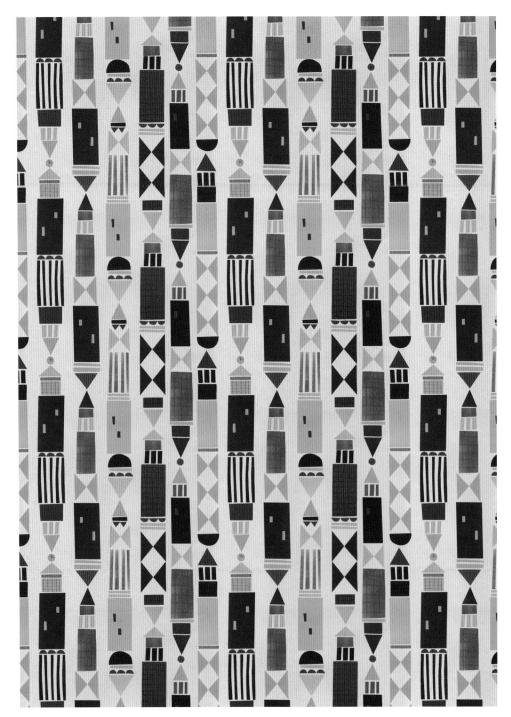

Figure 2.33 This pattern by Molly Jean Brown shows a colourful and balanced design, clearly evolving from the initial sketchbook work and motif testing. The collage was scanned into a computer and digitally manipulated into the repeating pattern, whilst retaining the collage look of the artwork.

Figure 2.34 Hannah Whitehouse creates drawings of floral forms to build her patterns before scanning the artwork for digital files. By hand-drawing and colouring the motifs as arrangements of flowers and foliage, the motifs are designed to work together from the start, with negative shapes and sizes of flower heads considered in relation to each other. In the repeating pattern Whitehouse has digitally manipulated the original bouquet, mirroring the motifs to face left and right to provide visual movement and flow.

Figure 2.35a *Festival* by Mini Moderns celebrates the 1951 Festival of Britain and includes the landmarks on the South Bank in London associated with the festival. Illustrated here are the individually drawn motifs.

Figure 2.35b The black and white drawn motifs were scanned in to become digital artwork and constructed into a repeating pattern with colours added using design software.

Figure 2.35c Here is the final result of the design process for *Festival* in an interior styling shot, accompanied by accessories featuring the *Net and Ball* pattern, originally designed in 1951 by Peter Moro and Leslie Martin for the Royal Festival Hall carpet and reissued by Mini Moderns in collaboration with Southbank Centre.

Figure 2.35d A further design, *Pavilion*, was created by Mini Moderns using elements of their *Festival* pattern. This spot design is an example of a design coordinate, as it works with the main design.

Market level can influence the level of detail in the artwork and **complexity** of the design; the more complex, usually the higher the market level. The number of colours to be printed (for non-digital printing) and fabric choices will also relate to the market level. Each colour printed adds cost, and superior cloth will be expected in the luxury market.

market level — *the position in the market, such as discount store, high street store or luxury market, dictated by the cost of the product and brand positioning;*

complexity — *the intricacy or number of motifs / elements in a pattern design.*

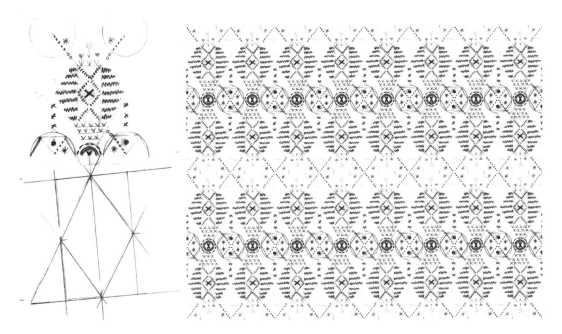

Figure 2.36 Here Kate Farley began with one tile and tested the repetition of the tile at the early stages of the design journey. Developing the overall rhythm of a repeat pattern can take lots of trial and error.

Repeat and rhythm

Usually, industry requires artwork to repeat both for ease of production and also for the application of a design to a large surface area. There are a number of repeat structures designers can use. Throughout the design process it is worth testing how the design will repeat to ensure that the overall flow and composition of individual elements continues to work when multiplied.

The area that repeats is referred to as the **tile** or **block**, and how far you move the next tile down beside the first one is referred to as the **drop**.

> **tile** — *the repeat unit of a design, also referred to as **block**;*
>
> **drop** — *the vertical distance at which a tile is repeated in relation to the tile beside it;*

> **full-drop** — *each tile of artwork is placed adjacent in a vertical and horizontal grid;*
>
> **half-drop** — *each tile is dropped half the depth of the tile lower than the one beside it;*
>
> **step-repeat** — *the tile is dropped less than half the distance of the neighbouring tile; this can be a third-drop, or similar;*
>
> **brick** — *a true brick repeat is offset horizontally, as bricklayers build walls;*
>
> **fake-drop** — *placing motifs in a full-drop design, where a half-drop would repeat, tricking the eye by suggesting the zig-zag of a half-drop.*

The most basic repeat method is the **full-drop**, the same motifs repeating inline both vertically and horizontally. The whole of the tile is copied next to and immediately below and above the original tile. Within the block nothing need repeat, but planning the joins between tiles is crucial for a flowing repeat. A stripe design will need to repeat as a tile in the same way as a geometric or floral to ensure the design can be printed, so there will be a point when the top of the tile matches the bottom even if it appears seamless.

When creating repeating designs there will be lots of measuring, and accuracy will be required to ensure tiles fit perfectly together. In planning a pattern, it is wise to sketch, trace, photocopy or scan the original and lay it out in the intended repeat structure to see how the rhythm of the design changes, so that positioning of the motifs can be adapted. A repeat can appear obvious if the pattern features few motifs as they will repeat often.

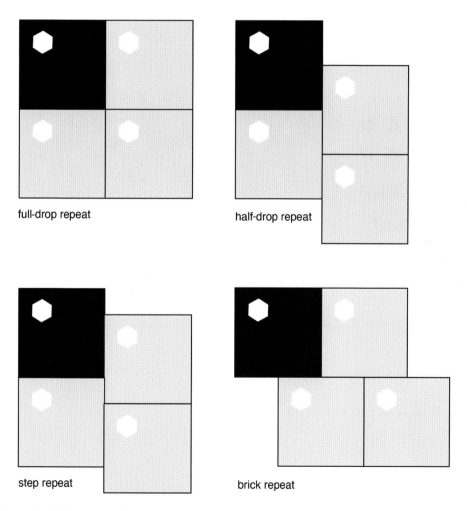

full-drop repeat

half-drop repeat

step repeat

brick repeat

Figure 2.37 This diagram illustrates the most common repeat systems used today.

Figure 2.38 The different rhythms created from placing a single tile as a full-drop and half-drop can be seen here.

Figure 2.39 This diagram illustrates how a single tile can be manipulated to create new, larger repeat tiles to provide more interesting rhythms. The original tile (A) is copied and rotated to form a new larger tile. This new tile is repeated in a full-drop structure. As the original motifs are rotated in the larger tile, there is a greater sense of movement, in comparison to the original single tile in repeat, as shown above.

Figure 2.40 This diagram from Jules McKeown of The Pattern Social shows the process of making a 'cut-through' to test the layout of motifs in a block as a full-drop repeating tile: Draw the motifs across the tile, avoiding the edges of the paper. Cut the tile in half vertically, switch the sides and tape together on the reverse. Add new motifs in any gaps along the new central seam. Cut the tile in half across the design. Switch the sides and tape together on the reverse. Add motifs to any awkward spaces. The tile now repeats on all sides as a full-drop.

Figure 2.40

Figure 2.41 *Sanna*, from Bluebellgray, is an all-over abstract design. To show how the design repeats there are four repeat tiles presented in this diagram with small gaps between the tiles. The motifs spread seamlessly when repeated across the fabric. There is another carefully considered element here, creating a design that appears to be a half-drop; this is called a fake-drop. The lower green motif in the tile is a duplicate of the higher one, rotated slightly and placed offset from the higher one. A zig-zag rhythm is created in the repeating pattern, similar to the half-drop repeat structure.

Figure 2.42 This design repeats as a full-drop but appears to be a half-drop repeat. Molly Jean Brown has duplicated one motif, the red snail shell on blue, and rotated it before dropping it into the pattern near to the point a half-drop would appear, creating the zig-zag of a half-drop within a full-drop tile.

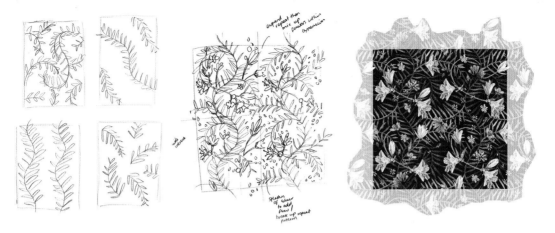

Figure 2.43 Molly Brown has created a tile composition of motifs and repeated it to create a 2 x 2 block. Inside the new larger block there are further alterations of individual motifs, creating a more varied composition in the larger repeating tile. Starting with small blocks and building them to make larger repeat tiles with variations is a useful way of building confidence with repeating patterns.

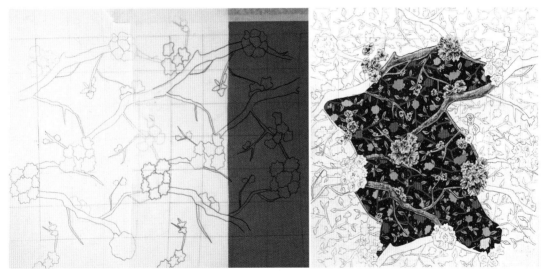

Figure 2.44 Drawing a pattern repeat as a final artwork will require careful measuring and planning. Here Molly Brown is testing the motifs in a full-drop repeat using a drawn grid and tracing paper, before she draws and finally paints the fully coloured artwork. This artwork, although not a square or rectangle, can be scanned for digital printing, as the piece will fit as a jigsaw for repeating, hiding any joins in the tiling. A rectangular repeat tile can then be digitally created. This method was used long before computers and can be seen in the design drawings of William Morris and his peers. The jigsaw repeat tile is still used for screen printing designs today, known as the *cut-through*.

The **half-drop** repeat structure is often used in interiors, as the resulting offset tiles provide a more flowing result with a diagonal rhythm over a room of wallpaper or large area of curtains. If the drop is a third of a drop or quarter-drop, it is known as a **step-repeat**. With an understanding of how patterns repeat to create different rhythms the use of complex motifs inside the tile can be explored. There are some very straightforward patterns on the market with only one motif repeating one after another; it takes skill and experience to build complex patterns that offer greater visual interest. Good designers will ensure their portfolio highlights a range of repeat and pattern structures they are capable of.

Figure 2.45 Woodchip & Magnolia have interpreted the traditional woven damask pattern with large symmetrical stylized florals in *Fearless Damask*, a digitally printed wallpaper. An alternating rhythm is provided by the half-drop repeat.

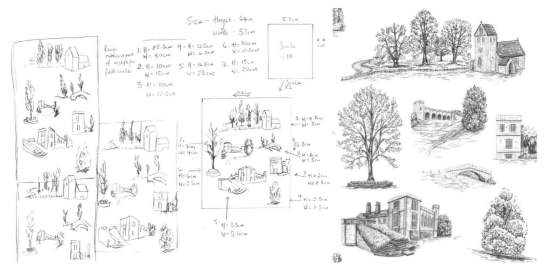

Figure 2.46a Maisie Miller sketched the rhythm of her pattern, *Ilam Park*, using a half-drop repeat structure, helping her to place the motifs appropriately in the repeat tile as she drew them.

Figure 2.46b In Maisie Miller's final half-drop repeating design of *Ilam Park*, visual interest is created by varied direction and angles of trees and buildings, leading the viewer through the pattern.

Figure 2.47 Containing a strong sense of rhythm in the linocut motifs, *The Harvest Hare* pattern by Mark Hearld for St Jude's illustrates the half-drop repeat on wallpaper. The varying printed texture, shifting directions that the creatures face and tonal variation ensure the eye is kept moving across the design.

Repeat tile sizes can vary considerably. A pattern repeat in a fashion context may be far smaller than in designs for interiors as the area to cover in a room is likely to be substantially larger than the body. A repeat tile for upholstery may be 64 x 64 cm, while wallpaper repeat tiles will often be 52 cm wide as determined by the width of the paper being printed (but could be longer). In fashion, designs for men's shirting, for example, may be smaller than 10 x 10 cm, but for a maxi dress the repeat could be larger. When pattern matching at seams for joining fabric (in any context) a smaller repeat tile reduces waste as the motif appears at more regular intervals. It is important to consider that a client may have particular repeat size requirements for manufacturing as this will affect the design process.

Designing in repeat for wallpapers requires further consideration as the standard wallpaper roll width is 52 cm wide and 10 metres long.

Figure 2.48 This stripe design wallpaper, *Backgammon* by Mini Moderns, features a half-drop repeat, identifiable by the alternating placement of circles with rings.

Figures 2.49a & 2.49b *Newsprint* wallpaper by Tracy Kendall is screen printed, enabling a more flexible repeat drop compared to traditional processes such as flexographic or surface printing that are governed by the circumference of the roller. This design repeats at every 90 cm. There are two colourways here, both single-colour designs. Kendall is renowned for her alternative wallpaper featuring sequins, and also prints single motifs on wallpaper, as non-repeating designs.

In commercial wallpaper production, alongside digital printing, processes such as flexographic printing and surface printing are employed. Rollers carry the design on the roller surface, limiting a tile size by the circumference of the roller. Common tile sizes are therefore 52 cm wide and between 53 and 68 cm high. This governs the repeat tile size, and, therefore, artwork preparation. Full-drops, half-drops or step-repeats can all be employed. Each colour will require different rollers. Digital printing can enable a designer to create any repeat drop length, but the 52 cm width is still most common, although there are manufacturers who specialize in printing extra

wide wallpaper. It is also important to ensure motifs are cut through on the edge of the wallpaper width to enable the rolls to be pattern matched using those motifs during installation.

When designing patterns for interiors it is important to consider how the pattern works across large surface areas; some areas can demand too much attention or feel unbalanced and require editing. Some patterns appear to seamlessly flow and spread while others appear bolder with the repeat tile more apparent. There are a number of considerations that affect the overall visual rhythm of a design created when put in repeat that should be part of an ongoing list throughout the process.

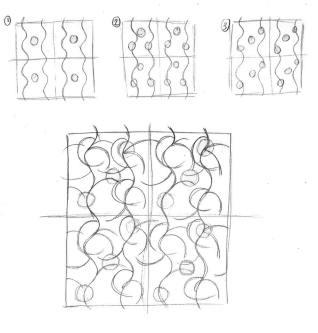

Figure 2.50 Molly Brown's diagrams explore the rhythms created by motifs for spot patterns in single tiles and as repeating patterns. With the third example a strong diagonal row of dots appears across the larger repeating area.

When designing a spot pattern, it is useful to test the placement of motifs for the resulting repeat rhythms. A spot design can enable a scattered, random composition, but it takes planning to make that impression. Some spot structures generate diagonal stripes of motifs too.

DIRECTION OF FLOW

Varying the direction individual motifs face can alter a design considerably. If a zoo-inspired pattern has all the animals facing the same way the overall impression will be single direction, and the eyes will move that way. A pattern including animal motifs facing different ways will offer a greater sense of dynamism and movement, providing a more varied rhythm. The pattern can appear to include a conversation between the motifs, even if it is not a traditional conversational print. Alternatively, one motif facing a different direction, acting as the odd one out, can offer visual interest. As the rhythms and flow of a design will be exaggerated across a large wall it is important to test a variety of directions for the motifs in relation to each other in the repeat tile. When making a multi-directional design it can help to rotate the paper or digital file as you place the elements of the design to stop having a top and bottom of the design.

Linking motifs can achieve a sense of flow and movement. Flowing ribbons or flocks of flying birds can appear to drift through a pattern,

Figure 2.51 In *Whitby - High Tide* by Mini Moderns a flowing rhythm established by the waves of the sea carries the fishing boats while gulls fly in the wind. The waves create visual movement as horizontal ribbons lead the eye to and fro.

leading the eye to other motifs. By varying the length of motifs, the longer elements spread interest across the design.

MOTIF SHAPE

A range of motifs of differing shapes will lead to varied rhythm as they each have a different purpose. Long thin motifs, circles and spiky stars guide the eye in and around a pattern, directing attention from one area to another. A circle can hold attention as it is a contained shape that creates a pause. In contrast, a star has spikes that guide the eye out from the points, and across to other motifs. Long motifs provide direction, carving up negative space, linking with other motifs.

A variety of motifs in a pattern creates a generous design; a design containing multiple, varied elements also has the potential to command a higher price. It takes time to perfect the harmonious relationship of each element in a design; practice helps!

SCALE AND PROPORTION

When the motifs in a pattern are differing in size there is more to hold attention. Simply increasing the scale of elements can create dynamic designs that inject tension and excitement into a room.

Some shapes can be used to dominate as key visuals, whilst other motifs are connectors, creating a network of visual interest. The eye will seek differences and similarities across a pattern, so a mix-and-match approach can provide energy.

Figure 2.52 *DazzleCam 2* by Quirk & Rescue illustrates how motifs of different shapes and lengths create flow and dynamic rhythms. In this full-drop repeat the uniformly placed yellow arrows lead the eye rightwards, but the grey zig-zag lines return attention to the black, blue and white shapes, linking the entire pattern.

Figures 2.53a & 2.53b This scattered repeating design by Hannah Whitehouse includes multi-directional flower heads at varying scales. The tonal variation in each cluster of motifs adds to the visual depth of the design, despite the neutral background.

COLOUR AND TONE

Varying colour and tone of motifs will make differing contributions to catch attention. A motif large but pale in colour may appear less dominant than a smaller motif in a stronger colour. Making these changes demonstrates skill and consideration and can result in designs appearing far more complex. Harmonious colours can provide a calming spirit in an interior space, whilst clashing colours in contrasting tones can offer drama and energy.

Figure 2.54a Molly Brown's diagram illustrates the testing of colour blocks within a tile, and how the colours work when the tile is repeated as a full-drop.

Figure 2.54b Here is the final design of varied colour blocks positioned with consideration to provide visual interest. Note the way the motifs have been manipulated to create a larger repeat tile, by rotating or mirroring some of the motifs from their original position, disrupting the expected repeating rhythm.

Colour in design

Colour is a vital ingredient in pattern design, working with the motifs and pattern structure to provide mood and spirit. Sometimes colours may come from the subject matter of the design, such as the colour of flowers or animals, but often the colours will be altered to suit the full pattern and fabric collection, coordinating

Figure 2.55 Creating a colour palette can be inspired by anything, but often the natural world is a good place to start. Learning to match colours is a vital skill in the textile industry, particularly for colourists working in manufacturing, ensuring colour matches across interior surface materials and products.

with other furnishing products and accessories, following trends or customer expectations. A **colour palette** has no fixed numbers of colours but six to eight would be a good starting point. Some collections will feature a colour palette of fourteen colours, but each design may only employ a fraction of the palette. The number of colours can also depend on how the pattern will

be produced; a screen-printed design requires a different screen for each colour so can be costly. A design could be made of only two colours—the background and one printed colour—whilst luxury cloth may use twelve to fourteen colours. If a design is digitally printed, colour palettes are not limited so designs could be made up of hundreds of different colours. However, a

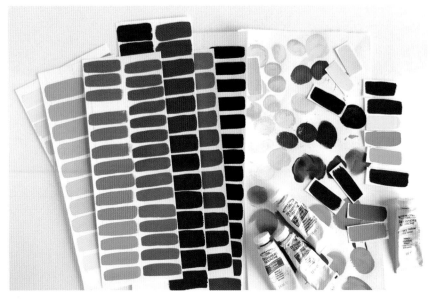

Figure 2.56 Painting gouache colour chips is a good way to play with and explore colour. Traditionally, gouache was used to paint design artwork as the colours are opaque and mix well, providing a solid colour. Mixing colour using paint or inks allows you to see how colours are made and adapted by adding other hues. The colour chips can be cut up and compiled into palettes for further testing and exploration.

designer is likely to design a colour palette stating the key colours to guide the mood of the design and identify **accent** colours. When establishing a colour palette, it is sensible to test differing proportions of each colour to ensure flexibility in how the colours can be used in combination.

COLOUR TERMINOLOGY

colour palette — *a formal selection of colours working together;*

accent — *a statement colour;*

hue — *the colour;*

tint — *white added to the original **hue**;*

shade — *black added to the original **hue**;*

neutrals — *these are more low-key colours in a **palette** holding together the brighter or darker **hues**, for example: creams, beiges and greys;*

monochrome — *a palette of colour with limited variation in **hue** (e.g. black and white with greys);*

colourways — *an alternative **colour palette** for the original design; designs may be available in a number of colourways.*

Figures 2.57a & 2.57b A photograph has been used as inspiration to form colour palettes, one of equal colour proportion, and one with proportional colour selection based on the amount of each colour in the image. Adobe Photoshop was used to pick out colour and present them as swatches to form the palette. This is a good way to build palettes, testing the accent colours.

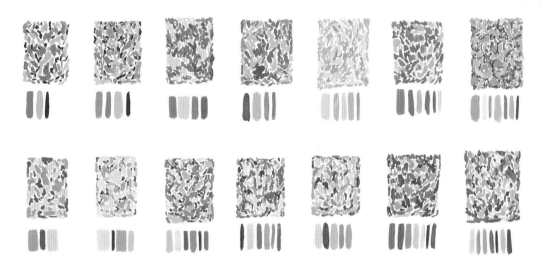

Figure 2.58 Maisie Miller has used gouache paint to test the colour relationships in a palette by creating small swatches. She has also tested different proportions of colour.

Each colour in a colour palette has a job to do. There may be bright **hues** providing cheerful accents to motifs; there are also likely to be mid-tones and darks offering tonal variation, depth and intensity. **Tints** and **shades** of colours can add interest. Mixing colours using gouache paint is a good way to learn the relationships between colours, manipulating the colour chips to test palettes. A colour palette can be very cheery right through to **monochrome**

Figure 2.59 Molly Brown's colour palette establishes a dramatic mood using highlights on the gentle motifs, supported by the visually heavier-weight colours of the saturated background and tonal foliage. The colour palette shows the proportional usage of each colour within the pattern.

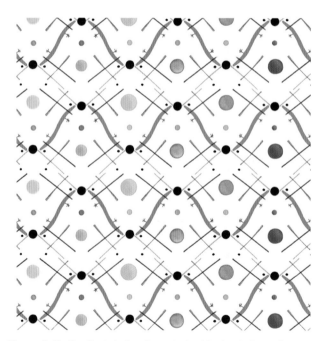

Figure 2.60 Ottoline's design, *Improvisation Number 1,* shows the successful use of tones of colour in relation to their size. The darker spots are smaller, in contrast to the larger spots in lighter tones, to balance the colour relationships across the pattern. The mid-tone lines link the separate motifs.

and practising working with colours outside of personal preference is useful experience for industry as clients frequently provide the palette.

Think of an interior colour scheme and consider what role each colour plays. **Neutrals** are important as they offer breathing space in a design, leaving bolder motifs to grab attention. No colour works in isolation, so always consider the roles colours play in relation to others in the palette: a mustard yellow may be bright in one colour palette, but neutral in another.

When creating a palette, inspiration may come from the drawn subject, or may be gathered from somewhere entirely different. It is useful to collect colour palettes that work together, including samples of fabric, paper or objects that enable testing of how each colour works in relation to others. Some designers follow a specific trend with a prescribed colour palette. With any palette you must explore the colours in combination and in smaller palettes to create contrast and variation in mood across several designs for the same

Figure 2.61 *Pleasure Gardens* by Mini Moderns employs a limited colour palette to provide balance. Motifs of varying sizes and shapes hold the colour differently, with stronger colours being used on small areas. The pale blue in the background links the brighter motifs, using negative and positive areas of clouds.

Figure 2.62 In this calming pattern, *Oak Tree* (Darkness colourway), Abigail Edwards has created the key motif, the branches and leaves, in white while the background holds the darker tone. Small acorns provide a warmer hue to attract attention. There are further colourways, including one with a white background, presenting a very different mood.

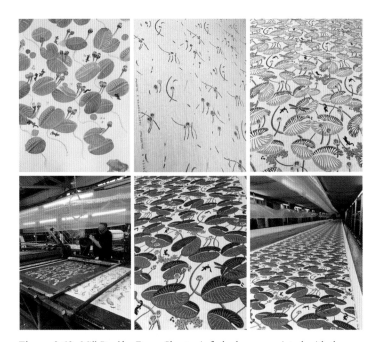

Figure 2.63 *Mill Pond* by Fanny Shorter is flatbed screen printed with the design being constructed by five separate screens, one for each colour. The first image is a painting of the design. The subsequent images show print production at IVOs, including Podge the Printer adding colour to the screen. If a final design is to be screen printed, it is useful to think of the artwork in layers of colour from the beginning.

project. Working with colours in varying proportions makes significantly different statements.

Within the design process it is important to test colours on various motifs to see the role colour can play. If motifs appear too dominant, they could be made smaller in size, or the colour lightened to make it less dominant in the overall design. Using the same colour on several motifs arranged across a design leads the eye between shapes, providing flow and movement.

The background must be given consideration as it holds the design together. Textured colour

Figure 2.64 Within a collection the patterns will showcase various visual qualities to contribute differing voices across the designs. This *Lilaea* collection by Clarissa Hulse for Harlequin showcases all-over and directional patterns; both the scale and colours of the motifs add further variation. A collection may be launched with very different colour palettes.

Figure 2.65 Angie Lewin's *Meadow's Edge* design comes in several colourways on a natural cloth. Each colourway of two colours is calming, but the accent colours enable the fabrics to work with differing interior colour schemes. You can read more about Angie Lewin's work in Chapter 3.

and negative shapes provide visual interest uniting the elements of a design. Adding shadows to motifs can give weight and solidity. Outlines to shapes must also be considered. Black outlines are too often the default choice for designers learning to make pattern, but black can appear lifeless and uninteresting; other line colours may suit the overall palette much better.

A **colourway** is the design in different colour palettes. Colourways were traditionally likely to retain the tonal values of the motifs, but this is not necessarily true today, resulting in some considerably contrasting results.

Digital design: An introduction

This section introduces basic considerations when designing patterns digitally. Working on a computer can speed up the design process but it remains vital to generate high-quality ingredients. Designing digitally enables swift editing of motifs, easy exploration of colour and scale, and quick repeat construction.

Traditionally created artwork (drawings, paintings, etc.) can be scanned into digital form for computer editing. There are different approaches to working with scanned artwork. Motifs can be drawn and scanned in individually, often black on white paper. The white can be removed from the digital file easily with selection and editing tools to leave black lines and textures on editable layers where colours can be edited and compositions adjusted. Motifs can be overlapped and layered accordingly. Alternatively, a repeating tile design can be created by hand on white paper and scanned so it can be cleaned up and prepared for production digitally. Some designers prefer a combination of the two approaches, scanning in clusters of motifs and editing before printing. Working on large and complex designs on a small screen can be problematic, as the overall design cannot be viewed in one go.

When translating drawings into digital files it is crucial to create a file that is of high enough quality for the intended purpose, the scale and application of the design. The quality of a digital image file is defined by the number of **dots per inch** (**dpi**), referred to as the **resolution** of the image in both

Figure 2.66 Painted motifs are manipulated digitally to create the repeating artwork for this digitally printed wallpaper, *Ava Marika* by Woodchip & Magnolia.

Figure 2.67 Inspired by the patterns of Lucienne Day, Kirath Ghundoo works digitally to create designs such as *Lucienne*, a process entirely unthinkable at the time Day herself was designing.

Figure 2.68 This print for bedding by Bluebellgray relies on digital design software and printing. As long as the artwork is scanned in at a high resolution the motifs can be enlarged and manipulated simply for digital printing.

scanning and printing artwork. If the **resolution** of a file is too low the image will appear **pixilated** and poor quality when printed; this can only be solved by re-scanning the artwork at a higher resolution. High resolution scanning results in larger digital files as more information is gathered during the scan; larger files can slow down working but quality cannot be added to poor images, so it is worth getting it right first time.

Usually, when preparing a file for digital printing on paper or fabric at the same size as the original, it should be scanned at 300 dpi. If artwork is to be printed at a larger scale, a higher resolution scan is needed to ensure no pixilation occurs at the larger size. A good rule of thumb is 100 dpi x each size increase: an output four times

the size of the original will need to be scanned at 400 dpi at least. The printer or manufacturer will know what they require, and this will dictate settings.

Artwork created on a computer can be developed using **raster graphics** software such as Adobe Photoshop, or a **vector-based** program such as Adobe Illustrator. Pixel-based software feels more like traditional drawing: pixels can be drawn, selected, moved, aligned and transformed to build patterns. Details can also be rubbed out with an eraser tool as would be done on paper. In contrast, in vector-based software, shapes and outlines are created and edited via anchor points and intersections; this requires familiarization and practice. A major benefit of vector-based artwork is that it can be enlarged without loss of quality through pixilation, particularly useful for large-scale artworks for interior and exterior projects.

Some designers create artwork entirely digitally. Drawing digitally using a mouse or graphics tablet

Figure 2.69 Kirath Ghundoo's wallpapers, including *Jazz Tartan*, are digitally created, from initial sketches to final outcome using Adobe Illustrator, ready for digitally printing. Digital manufacture means that the number of colours in the design can be unlimited.

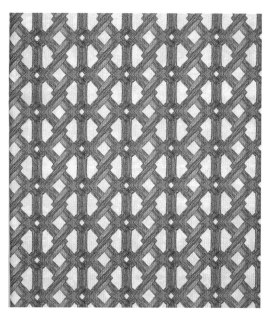

Figure 2.70 Eva Sonaike hand-draws all the components for the pattern and then scans the artwork to digitally edit the file in Adobe Photoshop. She puts the design into repeat and ensures the scale is correct before final print production.

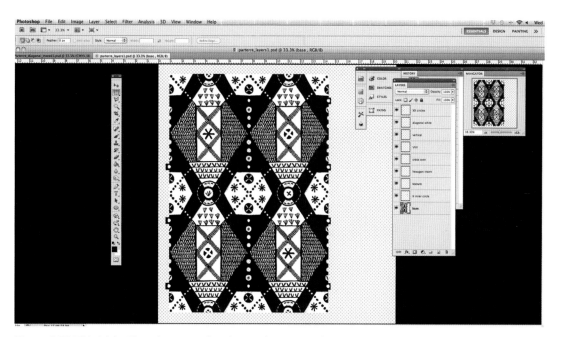

Figure 2.71 This Adobe Photoshop screenshot shows a design made for Parterre, by Kate Farley. Careful management of layers by naming, merging and linking saves time.

to create the design makes for easy editing of scale and colour and the results can be printed as required. Via drawing and editing tools the line quality can be adjusted, textures added, filters applied and motifs duplicated, enabling a design to be easily tested. Motifs can be adjusted using transforming commands (e.g. rotate, mirror, flip, align). It is easy to copy and paste lots of the same motifs to fill a design area; however, motifs should retain interest and offer variation. Being generous with varying motifs allows designs to become stronger. It is easy to get the computer to do the repetitive work, but it may compromise design quality if you ignore the considerations covered earlier in this chapter.

Working digitally requires good organizational skills; it is very easy to quickly create multiple copies of a motif, but each time an iteration of the motif is added a new 'layer' is formed in the file. Naming the separate layers will ensure motifs are edited as intended. Layer options within the editing software permit further control to merge, lock, hide or link layers, allowing precise and efficient editing. It takes discipline to manage the layers well to be an efficient digital designer.

There are tools in editing software to help put designs in repeat: for example, the *offset* tool and *pattern preview* option in Adobe Photoshop are ideal means for testing the repeating rhythms before committing to making a paper cut-through or creating the final artwork. It is simple to repeat a motif but far harder to make an interesting pattern that repeats, so it is important to take time to test and refine the repeat tile. Saving versions as the pattern is evolved allows for reflection on successes and failures. Some digital repeats can appear clunky—cutting

Figure 2.72 Original paintings consisting of many complex colour mixes can be scanned in to create digital designs, and the background paper removed. As more colours do not result in extra cost in digital print production designers can maintain the subtlety of colour, such as that found in watercolour, seen here in *Sanna* by Bluebellgray. Colours may still be separated in digital file layers to enable adjustments for colour matching and making new colourways.

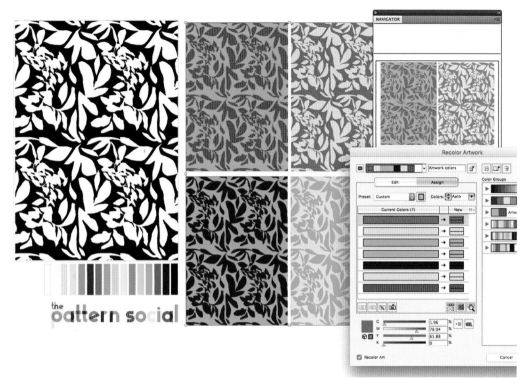

Figure 2.73 Here you can see colourways being created digitally by Jules McKeown of The Pattern Social. Computer software makes this process very quick, enabling designers to explore a range of colours in a defined palette across a collection of patterns.

through motifs, for example—resulting in basic and poor-quality rhythms. Remember, a strong pattern requires quality ingredients and visual interest, however it is created.

Digital colour:

Digital designing and printing enable designers to utilize thousands of colours in each piece of artwork, which is very different to traditional methods of printing. It is important to consider how a design is to be printed to ensure appropriate working at all stages of the digital design process.

Understanding how to calibrate software and adjust colour profiles is important, as is knowing what printer will be used to create the final print. A colour reference system, such as Pantone, allows designers to select a particular colour reference with a universal colour profile that can be matched by any printer across the world; this is particularly useful if a design needs to be matched to other materials. Colour swatch libraries can be accessed on some software, enabling designers to provide universal colour references for clients and manufacturers.

SAVING THE FILES

Digital artwork should be regularly saved, and files named for easy access. Keeping separate files with editable layers for key design stages will preserve developmental decisions and

Figure 2.74 Matching colours from the computer screen for printing on different surfaces can take time. Colour referencing systems such as Pantone allow your digital files to contain specific colour profiles to assist you in working with manufacturers across hard surface materials such as laminate, vinyl and tiles as well as fabric and wallpaper. Construct collection, by Kate Farley.

allows return to earlier outcomes. Flattening layered artwork and reducing resolution specification creates smaller files for quick print-outs or to send to clients as work in progress updates, but when buying final designs clients frequently request layered digital files of the artwork.

How much a computer is used to generate pattern is personal preference, and although analogue in output, screen printing often requires digital files to transfer artwork to the silkscreen. When considering commercial production, it is vital to understand how high-quality digital artwork files are prepared, including file types and colour modes. Files can be saved in different formats such as JPG, TIF, AI or EPS, and usually

the colour mode required is **RGB** or **CMYK**. Different companies have their preferences and working practices.

Digital terminology:
Resolution—There are **ppi** and **dpi** resolutions:

pixels per inch (ppi) refers to the digital size, the dimensions of a digital image on screen in a raster file, communicating the amount of information stored as pixels;

dots per inch (dpi) refers to the number of dots that will be printed out, determining if it can be a low- or high-quality print-out, and is also used in the scanning process to define the level of detail the artwork is scanned in at.

Pixilation—the image in raster files appears broken up and the individual pixels are visible, often caused by enlarging beyond the file capacity;

Raster graphics—artwork is arranged in a grid of pixels, often referred to as a bitmap. Each bit contains location and colour information that can be edited individually. These images are limited by how far they can be enlarged as the image will become pixilated. File extensions for raster files include .JPG and .TIF;

Vector-based—artwork is made up of paths containing points, anchors and curves along the paths. Shapes are contained by these paths defining the outlines and fill areas. Artwork can be enlarged without losing sharpness as there are no pixels, so this is useful for large-scale interiors artworks. File extensions for vector files include .AI and .EPS;

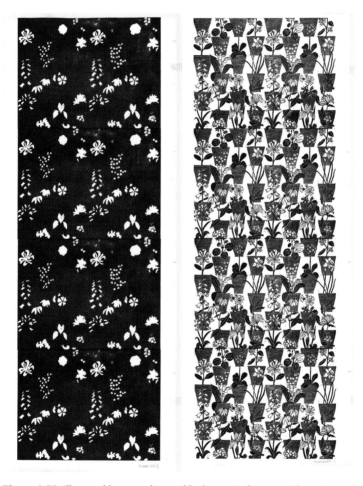

Figure 2.75 Illustrated here are the two blocks required to print *Flower Pots* by Marthe Armitage. The key details are on one block, and the background on the other. The two blocks will be different colours and will mix to create a new over-printed colour for the final wallpaper.

RGB—red, green, blue: the additive colour mode established by the mixing of coloured lights to create other colours on screens, but also a colour mode for digital design;

CMYK—cyan, magenta, yellow and black: the subtractive colour mode that references the commercial four-colour printing system to generate other colours through over-printing, also a colour mode for digital design.

Printing: Traditionally or digitally?

How final artwork is printed can determine how motifs are generated so it is important to consider what is the best printing process for reproducing the pattern. The printing method will affect the development of the colour palette too.

Figure 2.76 *Flower Pots* wallpaper by Marthe Armitage, from the two blocks in Figure 2.75.

Block printing as a production method is the oldest form of pattern printing. William Morris and his peers embraced the process during the Arts and Crafts movement and since then there have been several revivals of the process. There are designers block printing wallpapers and fabrics today and, as a result of the time-consuming nature of this method, they are usually comparatively expensive, small batch runs as each colour requires a separate block in the same way screen printing requires separate screens. (See the interview with Galbraith and Paul in Chapter 3.)

Screen printing includes flatbed and rotary printing, both with pigment pushed through a mesh with the design exposed on it. Artwork will be drawn, printed or painted on to separate layers of drafting film, and each one will be exposed through a light-sensitive emulsion to create the positive artwork on the screen. Artwork can also be scanned and digitally printed as opaque black positives, enabling manipulation of the artwork on the computer before printing. It is useful to test the layers and motif placement before exposing screens to print as it is costly to make changes later.

Figure 2.77 *Fig*, by Fanny Shorter, is a two-colour screen print, requiring two separate screens, one for each colour with artwork prepared accordingly. The silkscreen in the image features the design work for one of the colours, as a jigsaw piece, a cut-through for printing, that interlocks to produce repeating lengths of the design. Each screen is printed alternately on a long flat printing table, allowing adjacent prints to dry before the remaining jigsaw pieces are filled in. Subsequent colours are printed in the same way until the design is complete.

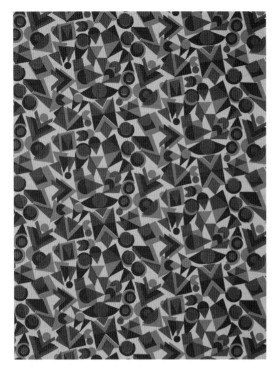

Figure 2.78 This lively geometric pattern by Peter and Linda Green for St Jude's illustrates the use of over-printing of colours to create an extra hue when screen or block printing. This reduces the cost of production by saving a screen and adds visual depth to the design.

A design needs to be colour separated to individual screens to provide each layer of the colour palette and these colours need to be kept in the right order for printing. For example, the shape of a cat is put on the bottom layer, and its eyes and collar put on second in a different colour (on a different screen). It is rather like woodblock printing in that one layer is printed at a time. Tracing paper can help to plan the order of layers as the pattern is built up.

As with block printing, artwork for screen printing can be designed so the colours will be over-printed rather than interlocking, thus creating additional colours without the additional expense of a further screen. For example, printing blue over red will give an extra purple in the design without the additional cost of a separate screen for purple. Fewer screens also mean less printing time. It is also useful to consider how negative shapes help define motifs, rather than resorting to additional colours.

A fundamental issue when designing and printing digitally is matching colours from what is seen on the computer screen to what comes out printed on paper or fabric. Matching hand-painted colour chips and material swatches with artwork on a backlit computer screen can be very difficult and, unlike screen printing, the colours are not mixed individually.

Digital printing software enables designs to be resized and edited far more quickly to adapt to commercial requirements. Developments in ink technology have led to opportunities to print on different materials, enabling versatile pattern applications on interior and exterior, hard and soft surfaces. Laser etching and cutting have been used in interior design applications for the last two decades and now 3D printing has become an exciting new territory for designers of pattern to explore.

Application and context

The design **application** refers to what the pattern is to be used for. Scale, complexity and rhythm of the motifs within the design will need to be considered in relation to the product and **context**. Patterns for interior applications can be designed at a scale significantly bigger than those for fashion contexts but will need to be considered in relation to the material they are printed on to.

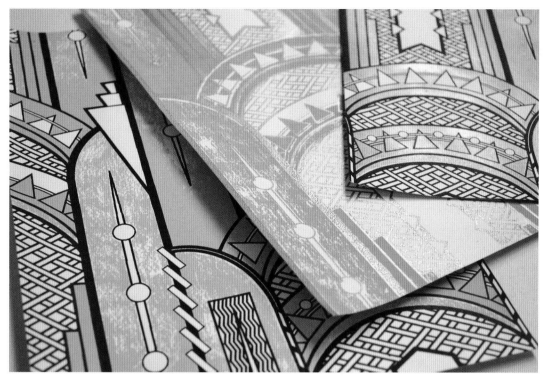

Figure 2.79 In *Onyx Skyline* wallpaper by Daniel Heath, the different colours that are screen printed to create the design, including a metallic pigment, can be identified. Surface treatments such as flocking and foiling can be applied by screen printing adhesives and then applying flock paper or foil sheets.

Figure 2.80 Four layers of colour—yellow, pink and two greens—are screen printed in this placement design by Florence Poppy Dennis. Additional colours are made when over-printing areas (pink printed over the yellow creates orange, for example), adding variety and depth to the palette.

Figure 2.81 *Cylinders* by Kit Miles uses large-scale circular motifs to make a striking impact on interior spaces.

Figure 2.82 Tamasyn Gambell's *Geometry* pattern collection features on a range of products, including lampshades, cushions and upholstery fabric.

Both the domestic (home) and contract markets (commercial environments such as hotels, restaurants and offices) utilize pattern, but the role of patterns can be significantly different according to the scale and function of the interior space. A wallcovering or curtain in a domestic setting may be used to define the home-owner's personal taste and provide comfort or drama. In a contract furnishing environment, such as a hotel lobby or doctor's waiting room, setting the patterns may be used for providing a sense of calm in a large space by using low-level visual textures or concealing heavy-use areas through heavily patterned surfaces, such as carpet and upholstery. Patterns and colours can be used to define zones in hospitality areas and may feature a company identity using brand logos.

There is a growing interest in bespoke pattern for interiors, as clients embrace their brand distinctiveness to set themselves apart. Digital production allows for short runs of printing without the traditional set-up costs. This enables designers to test the market and respond to customer feedback rather than investing heavily in production of fabrics or wallpapers that may be slow to sell.

By designing a pattern with a specific application in mind you can make sure your design works in relation to the surface it will be printed on and in relation to the form and function of the specific product. A pattern on a lampshade may be directional, with motifs the right way

Figure 2.83 Patterns can appear to work differently on contrasting substrates, so sampling can be crucial to ensure the material complements the pattern. Here the scale of printed lines is being sampled to ensure a good match on different fabrics, laminate and vinyl swatches of Kate Farley's *Threads* collection. Fine lines can be particularly challenging if printed on coarse woven fabric or textured surfaces as detail may be lost within the visual noise of the weave. Colour matching is also vital, especially if there is a sheen or metallic element to some surfaces as the light will make the colour appear significantly different.

up. The fabric will be held tightly over the shade structure so the drape of the fabric, the way the fabric hangs, is not so vital, but when designing for curtains the **drape** or **handle** of the fabric will affect the way the pattern is viewed. The amount of potential waste is important to consider too; ensuring repeat and pattern matching suits the product improves efficiency. Printing a design vertically along the fabric rather than horizontally is to print **railroad**, reducing the need for seams across upholstery, avoiding limitations in fabric width.

Figure 2.84 *Construct: Twist* by Kate Farley is applied to window film using digital printing to produce a contemporary version of the net curtain. Digital technology has enabled bespoke printing and fast customer service across hard and soft surfaces.

You can read more about design considerations in relation to materials and products in Neisha Crosland's interview in Chapter 3.

> **application** — *the product the pattern will be applied to;*
>
> **context** — *the environment a design is intended for, such as fashion, interior or automotive contexts;*
>
> **drape** — *the way the fabric hangs—see* **handle**;
>
> **handle** — *how the fabric feels, affecting how it* **drapes**;
>
> **railroad** — *to print vertically, rather than horizontally along the fabric, particularly useful for upholstery;*
>
> **substrate** — *the material being printed on (paper, fabric, vinyl, etc.).*

The choice of fabric, paper or other **substrate** the pattern will be printed on to affects how the pattern will be seen. Fine detailed designs printed on to a coarsely woven fabric may be difficult to read in relation to the visual noise of the warp and weft of the fabric. Some wallpapers have textured finishes that require consideration too, yet fabric with a smoother surface will allow finer detail to be seen. On a solid surface such as laminate the artwork will appear very flat, so this will need to be considered in the design development phase.

3
Design Process: Interviews

Emma J Shipley

Angie Lewin

Orla Kiely OBE

Sarah Campbell

Neisha Crosland

Timorous Beasties

Galbraith & Paul

Deborah Bowness

Eley Kishimoto

Figure 3.1 Emma J Shipley: EJS for Clarke and Clarke Frontier wallpaper.

Figure 3.2 Emma J Shipley: EJS bedding and cushions.

DESIGNER INTERVIEW

Emma J Shipley

Emma J Shipley is a luxury British lifestyle brand known for imaginative prints based on Emma's hand-drawn illustrations. Inspiration comes from the unique beauty of the natural world, exploring myths, legends and surreal fantasy. Creations include home furnishings, accessories and luxury scarves, all adorned in Emma's colourful and intricately drawn artworks. Each piece is made ethically, in the finest materials.

The label launched at London Fashion Week in 2012, after Emma graduated from the Royal College of Art. The famous boutique Browns launched Emma's graduate collection of printed scarves, and more recently Emma J Shipley has won the Emerging Brand prize at the WGSN Global Fashion Awards and the Newcomer Award at the UK Fashion & Textile Awards, presented by HRH Princess Anne. The brand is now stocked in some of the best department stores and boutiques around the world, including Liberty and Harrods in London.

REPEAT: How did you become a designer of pattern?

ES: I have always loved art and drawing, but once I started studying an art foundation course after A-levels, I realized I really loved taking my illustrations off the page and turning them into products that could be used and loved. This led me to study textiles, sending me down a pattern-maker path!

REPEAT: What is it about repeating patterns that excites you?

ES: There's something deeply satisfying about pattern; it's proven that the human brain is wired to look for patterns in everything. Creating patterns from scratch is an exciting process, where you never quite know how it will end up!

REPEAT: Can you explain briefly your preferred process of creating a pattern that repeats?

ES: I do a huge amount of research before starting any design; this usually involves travelling to a location where I can see wildlife in its natural habitat, taking photographs and making sketches. I also bring in other influences, such as films, books or exhibitions that are interesting me at that time. I start to bring together this varied research

Figure 3.3 Emma J Shipley: Emma and Luna portrait 2021.

Figure 3.4 Emma J Shipley: Amazon drawing WIP.

and find some themes within it, before creating mood boards and starting to sketch very rough ideas. I often use tracing paper when sketching initial repeats to see how designs are going to look, and making changes at this stage until I'm happy with the flow. I then start sketching out the final repeat on large paper, before refining, rubbing out sketch lines and drawing the final artwork, which can take up to two weeks.

REPEAT: You first launched textile designs for fashion accessories and garments—what was it about designing for interiors that appealed, and how does designing for fashion differ from interiors?

ES: I was always interested in designing for interiors, and produced wallpaper for my final collection at the Royal College of Art. I could see that my style of design, its very detailed nature and the time it took to create each design lent itself to interiors, where typically designs have more longevity and are much less seasonal than in fashion. I also created a scarf collection at RCA, and this was something that was easier for me to start out producing and

selling, which was successful, and so took me down more of a fashion route for a few years. When I had starting hiring a small team and had more capacity, I came back round to interiors and we launched a small collection at a trade show, which was instantly picked up by Liberty and Harrods.

REPEAT: How important is the end product / application when it comes to design decisions?

ES: Those considerations are all hugely important—for interiors you usually have to work to set repeat sizes, and while you can re-scale designs once you've made them, it certainly helps to bear this in mind from the start. Scale is something that can completely change a design and its impact—as well as its potential uses. Depending on how designs are produced, there may be restrictions (and cost implications!) on number of colours, although there have been huge steps forward in digital print manufacturing in the last few years.

REPEAT: What factors do you believe make a successful repeat pattern?

ES: I personally find patterns that occur in nature the most inspiring and successful. These stem from simple mathematical equations, studied by many people over the years, including Plato and Aristotle in the time of the ancient Greeks, and more recently, Alan Turing and Benoit Mandelbrot. While simple equations govern the formation of these patterns in nature, they are never exactly symmetrical and never repeat exactly. This inspires me to create unexpected elements to my repeats, such as subtle asymmetry, as I believe this makes patterns even more intriguing and pleasing to the human eye.

Figure 3.5 Emma J Shipley: Kruger throw.

Figure 3.6 Emma J Shipley: EJS Lynx cushions and throw.

REPEAT: Which designer of patterns inspires you?

ES: Evolution and nature is the ultimate pattern designer … And if we're talking human designers, then certainly William Morris, whose nature-inspired woodblock repeats have beautiful harmony and have stood the test of time. I tend not to look at contemporary designers in the textiles or interiors space too much, as I would rather focus on my own inspirations from outside the industry in order to create unique designs.

REPEAT: What advice can you share to inspire new designers of pattern for interiors?

ES: Find what you're really passionate about and focus on your own esoteric inspirations. Look outside the fields of pattern and interiors for inspiration. Consider what motivates you and what is unique about your work.

REPEAT: Please select one of your most successful repeating designs for interiors and talk us through how you developed the design.

ES: Zambezi is one of my favourite designs I've created. It was inspired by my travels in Botswana and Zimbabwe, as well as Jules Verne fantasy novels, eighteenth-century scientific diagrams and Platonic geometry. I wanted it to be a structured repeat with two vertical lines of symmetry, but, as inspired by patterns in nature, making each side of the symmetry not quite identical, and always adding unexpected details. I use tracing paper to trace the edges of my repeat tile as I sketch it out, to see the exact lines of repeat, but draw everything within the tile freehand, to give that balance I love between structure and unpredictability. Once I've sketched in the whole design I do another check with tracing paper along the edges where it will repeat, and see if any changes are needed to the placement of the motifs. I then start to draw more forcefully, adding details as I go. These often change through the drawing process, as I make decisions on the design as I draw. Once I've completed the drawing I scan it into the computer and work on multiple colourways, considering the end use of the design.

Figure 3.7 Emma J Shipley: research and design development, Zambezi design.

Figure 3.8 Emma J Shipley: research and design development, Zambezi design.

Figure 3.9 Emma J Shipley: EJS for Clarke and Clarke, Zambezi fabric.

Figure 3.10 Emma J Shipley: Zambezi cushion.

Figure 3.11 Emma J Shipley: EJS for Clarke and Clarke, Zambezi wallpaper.

DESIGNER INTERVIEW

Angie Lewin

ngie Lewin is a British printmaker whose hugely popular art works are inspired by both the saltmarshes of the North Norfolk coast and the landscape of the Scottish Highlands. Lewin depicts these contrasting environments and their native flora in intricately detailed wood engravings, linocuts, silkscreens, lithographs and collages. She is attracted to the relationships between plant communities on an intimate level and her still lifes often incorporate seedpods, grasses, flints and dried seaweed collected on walking and sketching trips.

As well as designing fabrics and stationery for St Jude's, which she runs with her husband Simon, she has completed commissions for Penguin, Faber, Conran Octopus, Merrell and Picador and has designed fabrics for Liberty.

REPEAT: Why are you a maker of patterns?

AL: There has always been a decorative quality to my work and I love the activity of printing

Figure 3.12 Angie Lewin: in the studio.

Figure 3.13 Angie Lewin: Dandelion I and II, detail.

Figure 3.14 Angie Lewin: Spey Path I, linocut.

and creating multiples of the same image or motif. I enjoy experimenting with these printed elements, collaging them in a variety of patterns and printing different colourways. As a print-maker, there is a practical need to limit the number of colours in an image because each one involves the cutting and printing of a separate block, and I enjoy the process of working with a restricted palette.

I study and draw the same plant forms over extended periods of time. It's a process that enables me to see pattern and variation and observe their essential structure, which I find a

Figure 3.15 Angie Lewin: 5 Trees wood engraving.

Figure 3.16 Angie Lewin: sketchbook drawing.

Figure 3.17 Angie Lewin: sketchbook drawing.

constant source of inspiration. Unique patterns occur in natural forms and, as I draw and redraw my subject, the geometry and subtle asymmetry slowly reveal themselves. I enjoy the way that different colourways and scales, positive and negative shapes and interlocking forms are the starting points for patterns.

REPEAT: What are the key ingredients of a successful repeat pattern?

AL: I find that often the most pleasing designs are made up of just one or two colours which exploit the balance of positive and negative. In a successful repeat, the individual elements of the pattern interlock or flow so that the eye travels freely, but finds pleasure in spotting the motifs. Conversely, a pattern that celebrates the way the repeat is constructed—like when the tiled repeat of the elements is a strong part of the design, for example—also works well. But I do find that usually less is more—a couple of my recent designs became stronger when I reduced the numbers of colours used.

REPEAT: Please talk us through your design process, from initial inspiration to final design.

AL: My starting point is generally the same, whether I am designing a textile / wallpaper

Figure 3.18 Angie Lewin: Nature Table.

pattern or working on a limited-edition print for an exhibition. I spend a great deal of time out walking and sketching in the landscape, studying plant forms and collecting natural objects to refer to in the studio. I develop my ideas in a sketchbook and I'll often look back through past sketchbooks for inspiration too.

As I work on these ideas, certain elements will start to appear that suggest a rhythm or a pattern—cutting a large lino separation for a limited-edition print may inspire an idea for a pattern, for example. When that happens, I make notes in my sketchbook to refer to at a later date.

When I'm specifically working on a pattern, I bear in mind the way it will be reproduced from the outset, which means considering the scale and any constraints in the number of colours I can use. At this stage, everything is being developed by hand—I cut the design in lino, then print and collage elements together. It's only once I've got the pattern to the final stage that the computer's used to ensure the repeat will work for commercial printing.

REPEAT: What difference does the product the pattern is intended for make to the design process?

AL: Whatever the end product, all my designs start out as a linocut, often in two or three colours. However, it's important to me that a pattern is designed specifically for the product it is to be applied to, whether that's a textile, wallpaper or ceramic. The size of screens, the width and circumference of print rollers and production costs are all important considerations, while the detail and scale of my artwork and the type of marks I make vary according to the nature of the print process and the materials to be used. Fine, stippled marks work well on ceramic but wouldn't print successfully on a coarse linen, for

Figure 3.19 Angie Lewin: Clover pattern sketch.

Figure 3.20 Angie Lewin: Clover fabric, shoreline colourway.

example. The scale of the repeat is very important too—a design for a large repeat wallpaper mustn't be overpowering or, conversely, too small and fussy.

REPEAT: What is your earliest pattern memory?

AL: I remember certain fabrics around the house when I was very young, especially my inherited bedroom curtains which would've been a 1950s' design. As a child, I spent much of my time drawing and even then I would concentrate on the same subject, so my sketchbook would be filled with pages of rows of ducks, for example. When I was very small, I also remember a kitchen drawer filled with bits and pieces—old junk like nuts and bolts, pencils, marbles and tiddlywinks which I would lay out in endlessly different patterns.

REPEAT: Which pattern maker, past or present, do you most admire and why?

AL: Eric Ravilious. I'm most inspired by artists who also work as designers, and Ravilious stands out in particular as his own style was always so clearly evident in his commissioned work. The sophistication and craftsmanship of his watercolours, lithographs and wood engravings translated perfectly, whatever product he was designing for. As a printmaker he understood how to make one- or two-colour designs work perfectly and the translation of his soft drawn line on to Wedgwood ceramics is effortless. He was adaptable,

Figure 3.21a Angie Lewin: Hedgerow, detail.

Figure 3.21b Angie Lewin: Hedgerow linen.

designing ceramics, glass, wallpaper and fabric. But he was also a war artist, a fine illustrator and mural painter. His skill was to always retain his own style and colour palette in whatever he designed.

REPEAT: What advice can you share to inspire new designers of pattern for interiors?

AL: Having a broad range of influences is important, and is developed by looking at the work of artists, designers and makers in widely differing media. I find that music and writing are also influences, although it's hard to define how they are present in my work; they are a part of my working process. Observing the natural world by walking and sketching in the landscape is also vital to me. All these elements may often seem unrelated but by making associations between them your work will be a reflection of yourself. Even if you typically work on the computer, do experiment with more analogue techniques, where the quality of materials will transform your ideas. Spend time with your designs in the studio or at home, pinning them up to get a sense of how scale and colour are working. Experimenting with scale by enlarging or reducing elements can radically change the mood and impact of a fabric or wallpaper. Some patterns work well when hung or draped in folds, creating a further abstract element to your fabric design, while others are suited to the flat surface of a wallpaper or blind, so this is good to bear in mind when working on ideas. Thinking about the kind of interior space that a pattern might be suitable for is important and can inspire how you progress the design.

Figure 3.22 Angie Lewin: By Green Bank screen print.

REPEAT: Please select one of your most successful repeating designs for interiors and talk us through how you developed the design. What were the considerations and changes that occurred in the process of designing it?

AL: My fabric Meadow's Edge is inspired by native grasses which are often overlooked in the landscape and in botanical art, despite them being an integral part of our countryside as well as being vital to wildlife. The flower heads are endlessly varied in scale and texture and I often include them in my prints and watercolours alongside

Figure 3.24 Angie Lewin: cutting the block for Meadow's Edge.

Figure 3.23 Angie Lewin: sketchbook drawing.

native wildflowers. I wanted to create an interior fabric that evoked the calm of an expanse of meadow grasses and the subtly muted colours of the different species. I began by looking back through my sketchbooks and then started developing pattern ideas. These seemed to inspire a vertical repeat and I enjoyed experimenting with the scale of the flower heads to create two different bands, one punctuated by a large, stylized grass and the other with smaller-scale grasses entwined with native great burnet. As with all my designs, I then cut and printed lino blocks to create the two-colour fabric.

Figure 3.25 Angie Lewin: Meadow's Edge interiors fabric, colourways.

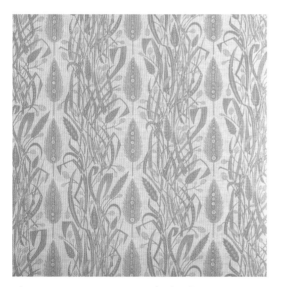

Figure 3.26 Angie Lewin: Meadow's Edge.

Figure 3.27 Angie Lewin: Meadow's Edge interiors fabric.

Figure 3.28 Orla Kiely: Fabric collection.

DESIGNER INTERVIEW

Orla Kiely OBE

rish-born, London-based designer Orla Kiely established the Orla Kiely brand with her husband in 1997, following time as a freelance designer and postgraduate study at the Royal College of Art, London. Regularly presenting ready-to-wear collections and accessories at London Fashion Week saw the brand grow quickly and it soon encompassed homeware and stationery and collaborations with international brands including Citroën.

Retro-inspired pattern, featuring bold colourful motifs of heavily stylized natural forms and geometric abstracts, has become instantly recognizable to an international audience. Orla Kiely was awarded an OBE in recognition of her services to business and the fashion industry in 2011.

Figure 3.29 Orla Kiely: working.

REPEAT: How did you become a designer of pattern?

OK: I was always drawn to pattern even as a young child. I adored the 70s' brown flowery wallpaper in my childhood bedroom and was lucky enough to have matching curtains and duvet!

I used to squint at it to work out where I could find the repeat.

Also, I loved art as a subject at school and was very keen on drawing and painting. It was my ambition to be a designer. It was in my foundation year at art school that I realized textile design existed as a thing and, as a fashion-loving teenager, I felt it was the perfect fit for me. Clearly, I never looked back!

REPEAT: What is it about repeating patterns that excites you?

OK: A successful repeat pattern has rhythm and flow; it's a perfect balance of the creative motif or element, the foundation of any pattern and how that plays with the background creating a harmonious and visually satisfying movement through the relationship of filled and open space. We build structures with elements that become so unified in their repetition that a multiple of any designed motif becomes stronger than one single element. They do not float but rather melt together.

Colour is another component here and plays an important role. The power of the colours used has a huge impact, and the process of experimenting with colour, applying and testing how they work together, to the final choices and decisions made, is vital to a successful outcome.

Figure 3.30 Orla Kiely: bags.

Figure 3.31 Orla Kiely: Nouveau Stem print

Figure 3.32 Orla Kiely: Botanica print.

REPEAT: Can you explain your preferred process of creating a pattern that repeats?

OK: I always start every design with the creation of the element at the heart of the repeat. It's a very graphic approach, but if the element is weak or unresolved, the repeat will never be successful. It is the main component, and we take time to design, refine and simplify. When the element is perfect, we put it into a variety of repeats to see which is best. At this stage, how close or far apart we want them spaced is instinctive, relying on our eyes to decide the final outcome.

Then the colour work and working with a palette of colour, trying many different combinations of tones or opposites to work out which colours create harmony, complement or contrast, while always searching for the unexpected surprise of colour that immediately gives you a sense of joy and creative fulfilment.

Figure 3.33 Orla Kiely: Cut Stem print.

Figure 3.34 Orla Kiely: Cosmea print.

REPEAT: How important is the end product / application when it comes to design decisions you make during the process of designing pattern?

Scale, repeat size, number of colours all play a role and are all considered through the process. Repeat size can be a limitation as the scale gets bigger but we know we have to bear that in mind.

Scale changes everything and to me committing to scale is important. Big should mean big, and in an interiors context what seems big on the page can be very small in a room. It's always worth being open to that when deciding on scale.

REPEAT: What factors do you believe make a successful repeat pattern?

OK: It's always important to trust your instincts. A successful pattern is never a compromise. It has quality and intent and to me it is never over-worked or over-designed.

REPEAT: Which designer or company of pattern design inspires you?

OK: I love the textiles from the Modernist era. They experimented with scale, structure and colour. Few textile designers then were household names but at a time when we had a vibrant textile industry the cloth mills had teams of designers all creating amazing print and pattern designs. It continues to be a huge source of inspiration to me.

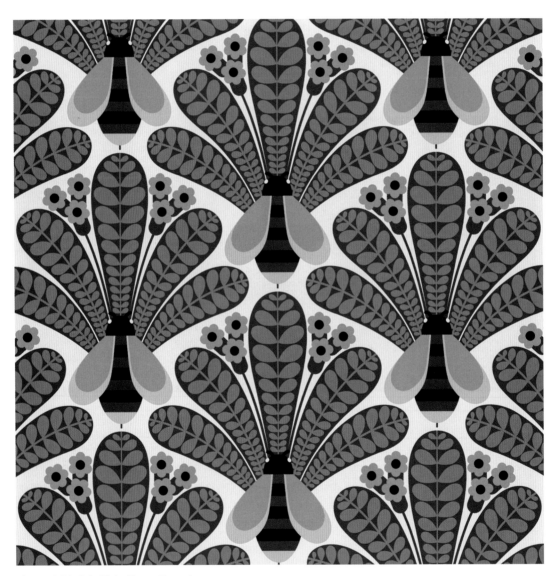

Figure 3.35 Orla Kiely: Honey Bee print.

REPEAT: What advice can you share to inspire new designers of pattern for interiors?

OK: Main points already covered.
Follow your instincts.
Don't be afraid to push the boundaries of scale.
And know when to stop.

REPEAT: Please select one of your most successful repeating designs for interiors and talk us through how you developed the design.

OK: Our stem design is a very good example. It flowed out of me on to the page with little effort, one of those moments when it was just right. A perfect combination of simplicity with a power and strength, a positive, uplifting rhythm that resonated with our audience from the very beginning.

We have had many iterations of stem and with that it has evolved. Over the years it has been perfected and refined. It is interesting to look at

Figure 3.36 Orla Kiely: Stem sketches.

our first stem alongside a more current one to spot the differences. The stems have all edged closer together, minimizing the ground space for more coverage. With all that, the leaves are the same, rounded rather than pointy, usually facing upwards, with continuity and growth, graphically aligned and centred, establishing a pattern we are told that is friendly, welcoming and always happy.

Figure 3.37 Orla Kiely: Stem CAD drawings.

Figure 3.38 Orla Kiely: Stem rug.

DESIGNER INTERVIEW

Sarah Campbell

Sarah Campbell has been painting patterns for textiles for well over fifty years; she co-founded the distinguished design company Collier Campbell with her late sister Susan Collier, formalizing their sisterly partnership. She now works on her own—making, teaching, writing and continuing to paint designs both for commercial production and as special commissions. She is the co-author, with Emma Shackleton, of *The Collier Campbell Archive: 50 Years of Passion in Pattern* (Ilex Press, 2012) and has published two other books: *The Art of Pattern* and *Dailies*, co-designed with Stafford Cliff.

Having started her career making designs for Liberty in the 1960s, she has worked in the industry consistently ever since, making decorative patterns for apparel, furnishing fabrics, wallpapers, patterned weaves, rugs and ceramics: from petite paisleys to glamorous florals to huge geometrics, from tiny 4-inch repeats for dress fabrics, to patterns 210 inches high for wide-width sheeting.

Over the years customers have included Bill Gibb, Yves St Laurent, Jaeger, Cacherel, Carline Charles, Habitat, John Lewis, M&S, Conran, Fischbacher, Museums & Galleries Ltd and, in the United States, Martex, WestPoint Stevens, Springs Industries, Imperial Wallcoverings, and more recently Michael Miller Fabrics, Free Spirit, West Elm and Anthropologie.

The mark of the hand has always been her starting point. Drawing and painting, mixing and matching colours, are fundamental to her design process, as is observation and an intuitive approach to balance and movement. She demands high standards for her work, whether using conventional or digital printing, and takes pride in producing the best results possible for herself and her clients.

Love of pattern and colour and an inventive freshness are the hallmarks of her work. Sarah Campbell uniquely combines expertise, experience, originality and joy.

Figure 3.39 Sarah Campbell: Flower Dance, *Fresh Picked* collection for Free Spirit.

Figure 3.40 Sarah Campbell.

SOFAS
à la carte

Figure 3.41 Sarah Campbell: Habitat catalogue featuring Rosscarbery sofa, 1987.

REPEAT: How did you become a designer of pattern?

SC: By chance really: my sister, Susan Collier, who was eight years my senior, had worked with Pat Albeck and Peter Rice as their general assistant before she'd married in 1961. As a new wife she began to build a career as a textile designer; she had her two daughters in very quick succession, and working in the evenings she built up a handful of customers—notably Richard Allan scarves and Liberty of London Prints. She found, with two babies, there wasn't enough time to do everything so she asked me to come and lend a hand—'You can draw, you can help.' So I did.

One of the jobs we were given from Liberty was to redraw old patterns using scraps from their archive—make them into new repeats, add colours perhaps, adapt them, and it was through doing this that I learnt what a pattern repeat was—and how very many ways there are to draw flowers even in a 4-inch half-drop!

I seemed to have a natural ability and interest in this, and throughout my sixth-form years, and then during my time at Chelsea School of Art (where I studied fine art and then graphic design) I was also working with Susan, inventing, tracing, painting patterns.

The first pattern of my own that I sold was to Mr Weiner, the producer at LOLP—a huge landscape drawing that I put up at my Diploma Show, to which he came! I put it into a repeat for furnishing fabric—everyone called it Weiner's Folly, but years and years later WestElm USA asked me to design a group of patterns based around it! As it happens, the idea of making a landscape into a flat design has always interested me.

After I left college I continued to work with Susan; my more inventive developments began to flourish. We worked together for about fifty years until she died in 2011. I continue alone.

REPEAT: What is it about repeating patterns that excites you?

SC: Infinity!

There is comfort and reassurance in pattern—whether the cycle of the yearly seasons or the whirl on a snail's shell … in some ways my life has been measured out in the heartbeat of repetition.

I've been fortunate enough to have been able to revisit and rework the harmonies and dissonances of pattern, and to get to know its workings quite intimately. At its essence is the excitement of making these rhythms spring to life through form and colour, and to be able to pass them on.

REPEAT: Can you explain briefly your preferred process of creating a pattern that repeats?

SC: I should preface this with the observation that I see repeats everywhere and in everything! I always imagine how a repeat will work before I start. My usual process—I tend to start with a painted sketch, something I've drawn or painted that has some potential for the end use envisaged. I often draw myself a little sketch to indicate how I see the pattern developing, a sort of schema. I approach patterns according to their needs—an abstract, a geometric, a scenic, a floral can each demand different methods and I usually address the considerations of size, colours and end use at this time.

In principle, I measure out and draw the repeat area in pencil on paper large enough for me to extend the pattern to see how the repeat's working, and to give me enough artwork for me to cut off and keep a strip before I send the painting to the customer.

Figure 3.42 Sarah Campbell: Sea Holly, Michael Miller Fabrics, 2015.

Figure 3.43 Sarah Campbell: Garden Teabowl, *Fresh Picked* collection for Free Spirit.

I start with a tracing—usually using an H pencil on good-quality tracing paper. I rule out the repeat grid on the tracing paper too, and write the letter R on the top right-hand corner of both the trace and the artwork paper so I always know which side of the paper is which! The process of tracing lets me get to know the design better and to redraw details as I go. I choose an area of the painted sketch which I think is good and represents the pattern. Once traced, I put it down, using trace-through paper, over one corner of the repeat grid, bearing in mind the extent in relation to its development. With a floral or an abstract, I 'grow' the pattern on the paper, not on tracing paper or elsewhere, so it's a living thing, and a bit risky.

A geometric pattern is a different prospect, requiring a considerable amount of measuring and mathematical planning.

Once I've put the first area down, and seen where the repeats will come, I start to paint it in. I'll be looking constantly at the whole area, thinking about the balance and the parts of the pattern yet to be invented. When I have a fair bit painted, I'll trace down the parts that repeat and block them in with paint. I continue to build the pattern tracing down, painting, drawing, tracing, painting, drawing until the area is complete.

Figure 3.44 Sarah Campbell: starting a repeat pattern.

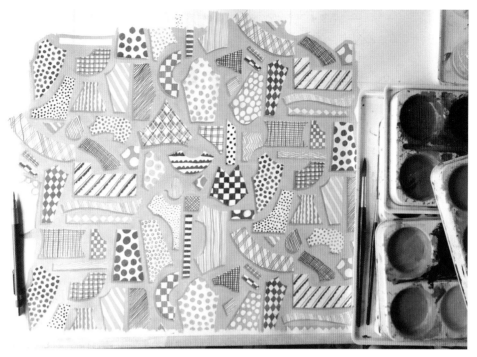

Figure 3.45 Sarah Campbell: the completed pattern, in repeat.

I take frequent breaks and evaluate how things are going. I often take photos as I go; we used always to take Polaroids of big repeats and put them together to see how things were going—for balance, inadvertent diagonals, etc.

REPEAT: Your design career spans a time that has embraced digital software and printing. How has this influenced your design process?

SC: Personally, I continue to think in terms of conventional printing for the most part—a conventional repeat size and a finite number of colours, mostly flat. Some of my clients still do print like this, and there's certainly a strong interest in screen and hand-printing currently. But digital printing offers the possibility of greater freedom in pattern size, and colour tone, texture

and number, and that can certainly be both exciting and delectable.

This isn't always the panacea it appears to be, and the rigour of conventional printing and pattern-repeat making has meaning and a certain discipline. I notice some very crude repeats and lazy and ugly (in my opinion) colourings walking about; subtlety can be sacrificed on the altar of speed. And scale, I imagine, may be difficult to appreciate through the medium of a small flat screen …

Printing digitally also gives one the chance to do very small runs. So I've been able to exploit these qualities in some of the printing I've done for my own company, and it's been useful. I've only really exploited the idea of tonality and endless colours in a couple of prints; I enjoyed

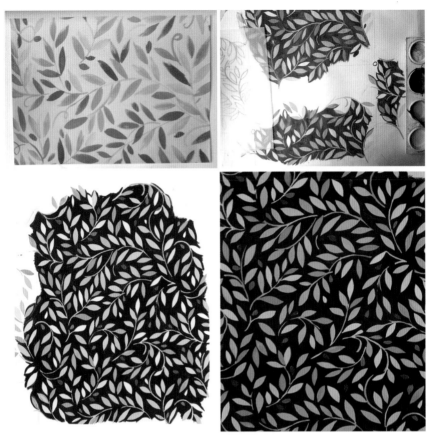

Figure 3.46a Sarah Campbell: initial repeat ideas; **b** Sarah Campbell: tracing the design to build up the repeat tile; **c** Sarah Campbell: full repeat, with colour alteration; **d** Sarah Campbell: final piece.

the experience and the results. But it's not cheap, and to do it well on good cloth with carefully balanced colours requires work and expertise. People say: 'Why don't you just print it digitally?' For me that little word 'just' is a danger signal!

REPEAT: Do you design the pattern with a specific end product / application in mind? When do you consider elements affected by context?

SC: Although I do many paintings, sketches and drawings with no obvious purpose, simply as ideas, explorations and entertainments, their scale, style and colour content are part of their purpose as patterns. A one-colour dot would have a different purpose to a full-colour floral, say, though they may well be designed to sit together in the same range.

I wouldn't do repeat work 'on spec', so to speak. I always need to consider my customer's needs, ambitions and limitations—financial, commercial and technical (and I may be my own customer!) so the scale, repeat size and drop, number of colours, method of printing, etc. have to be understood before I put an artwork in repeat. I habitually discuss the first sketches and ideas with the customer so we can decide these things together.

REPEAT: How do you know when you've designed a successful repeat pattern? Do you know when to stop?

SC: I think I can see when a repeat is successfully balanced—but whether the pattern itself will sell well and be successful commercially is another question! I'm never quite sure about that part.

Deadlines are a marvellous means to tell you when you've finished!

REPEAT: Which artist or designer inspires you?

SC: The world is full of amazing decorative textiles, traditional and contemporary, made in all sorts of ways—print, weave, embroidery, knit, lace, felt, stitch—and I'm constantly surprised and inspired by the ingenuity and skill of the makers, mostly unknown, often taken for granted. I take my hat off to them, past and present, working everywhere from the stoniest deserts to the

Figure 3.47 Sarah Campbell: Room with a View artwork.

lushest hillsides to the most modest villages to the concretest of cities.

REPEAT: What advice can you share to inspire new designers of pattern for interiors?

SC: I often wonder whether the design I'm working on is useful; that is to say, what does it bring that is worthwhile, what does it add to an environment—imagination, colour, texture, atmosphere, wit, ideas, generosity, a point of view? These are things worth considering, I think.

It's important that the designer is really involved with their work, to love the doing of it. I think one must respect the customer, listen to their needs and watch their reactions and be prepared to take them one or two steps further than they'd imagined.

Listen to your design, learn from your design, read your design and do everything as well as you can. You have the chance to be as generous and original as possible. And if it doesn't go well, learn from it but don't harass yourself—it's always

Figure 3.48 Sarah Campbell: Dahlia Garden, *Fresh Picked* collection for Free Spirit.

worth trying to understand why some things work and some don't.

REPEAT: Please select one of your most successful repeating designs for interiors and talk us through how you developed the design.

SC: I think one of my most enduring and well-loved designs for interiors must be Cote d'Azur. It's also one of the most recognizable—giving the lie to the old idea that bestsellers are always beige!

The first sketch, 1, was done in a typical rush of energy in about 1980, in response to my not having a summer holiday: 'Well, I'll paint one then!'

Strangely, my father saw that very rough sketch and said: 'That one's a winner.' I've often wondered how he knew. The design remained in a drawer until we secured a licence with Christian Fischbacher to make a range of six furnishing fabrics for them. Cote d'Azur became the linchpin. This range was called *Six Views*. This collection won the Design Council's award in 1984, and also the Duke of Edinburgh's design award that year—a first for textile design and for women.

The essence and energy of the first sketch needed to be formed into a repeating pattern that could be read and printed within a repeat size for furnishing fabric, where the width of the cloth is traditionally 54 inches and the largest vertical repeat at that time would have been 36 inches. In the first sketch the stage has been set—the motifs already had a semblance of repeat, there are birds in the skies, the sea in the distance and foliage among the architecture.

The essence of this design is a story—a holiday in the sun—which everyone can recognize. The play between planes, distance, literal and decorative motifs—now a tree, now the sky and a bird, now a pattern of water, balconies and awnings—is what makes the design. The colours of the original painting—bold primaries, tempered with a softer duck-egg and dusty pink, blue skies, cream ground and black—are part and parcel of its success. The essence and energy of the first sketch needed to be formed into a repeating pattern that could be read and printed.

The second sketch shows how the design is forming: a big repeat—27-inch wide half-dropping at 18 inches, which gives one complete picture across the width of the cloth. The colours—eight on quite a warm strong cream ground—have been mixed. The decision to have the bird, and just one, flying clearly in the blue sky, was a bold one; the idea of such a focus in a repeat is one I often counsel against. In this case it's the signature. Clearly in this sketch the details require work—I remember how difficult it was to decide just how real—or not—the trees needed to be!

The final 1982/3 painting shows that the decisions have been made. In fact, I no longer have this actual painting as it 'went missing' after it was shown at a Design Council exhibition in 1984! There's a tremendous mix of scale and pattern—diagonals, verticals, horizontals, waves, dots and criss-crosses all cooperating with the trees, bird and balconies. The cream ground manages to bring air and space.

The painting (below) is a later one done in 1991 for sheeting produced in the United States. The repeat area needed to be enlarged, so I painted it all anew as a 'square' repeat, adding a second bird where the original half-dropped bird would have been. No computers!

I often wonder why this design continues to be so loved. I think there are several reasons: first,

Figure 3.49 a Sarah Campbell: Cote d'Azur first sketch; **b** Sarah Campbell: Cote d'Azur initial pattern testing; **c** Sarah Campbell: Cote d'Azur repeat artwork; **d** Sarah Campbell: Cote d'Azur paper design for bedding.

it tells a story—a hopeful one of sun and trees and air and even freedom, that is immediately recognizable. The colours (and this was always by far the best-selling colourway) emphasize this. The pattern is expansive, yet the scale is not overwhelming. The repeat itself is one that bears scrutiny; it offers the chance to meander through the landscape, look at the sky, stand on the balcony and gaze out to sea, never sure where you might end up. In all, it's a generous pattern that gives pleasure.

Just a note—in 2011 I met with Christian Fischbacher's grandson, also Christian, who runs the company now. He told me that this design was a legend in the family—everyone had thought his grandfather was taking a terrible risk producing such an outspoken fabric! It was clearly a risk worth taking.

Figure 3.50 a Neisha Crosland: Shells, Bells, Waves; **b** Neisha Crosland: Flora, Fruit, Fauna; **c** Neisha Crosland: Scallops, Scales, Crescents; **d** Neisha Crosland: Criss Cross, Dots, Spots.

DESIGNER INTERVIEW

Neisha Crosland

N eisha Crosland is a pattern designer known for her well-balanced repeats of geometrics and flowers, unusual colour combinations and her ability to design patterns for a wide range of products, techniques and media.

Neisha trained in printed textiles at Camberwell School of Art, going on to the Royal College of Art in London. She was commissioned at her graduation show by Osborne & Little to design a collection for them. In 1994 she started her own eponymous textile label, designing and producing scarves for international fashionable shops. Today she works from her South London studio, designing pattern for tiles, rugs, wallpapers, fabrics, flooring, stationery and scarves. In 2006 she was honoured with a Royal Designer for Industry Distinction (RDI) and in 2017 the University of Arts London made her an Honorary Fellow. Her work is archived at the V&A and Museum of the Home, and her book *Life of a Pattern* was published in 2017.

Figure 3.51 Neisha Crosland.

REPEAT: What has been your journey to becoming a designer of pattern?

NC: It started at an early age, arranging pebbles and feathers and pressing flowers. I loved doing all the diagrams we had to do in biology and geography, and anything that involved illustrating a poem, map or the cross section of the digestive system or an atom. I remember, aged 11, doing a project on Nicholas Culpeper, the early seventeenth-century English botanist, herbalist, physician and astrologer, and I ended up copying his illustrations, then decorating them with homemade marbled mounts. I am very short-sighted but it was only diagnosed at 8 years old—so my early world was very blurry when looking at things from a distance but, close up, fine details of speckles and spots and lines on flower petals and leaves, for example, became wonderfully magnified. I lived in a polarized world of faraway blurry fuzzy shapes and close-up fine detail.

I ended up going to art school to do graphics even though I actually wanted to do fine art, but a strict and protective father persuaded me otherwise, worrying about the job prospects or lack of them with a fine art degree. My eureka moment came when I found myself lost in the Ottoman Empire textile gallery at the V&A, surrounded by fifteenth- and sixteenth-century fabrics. Dots, crescents, tulip heads, repeating

Figure 3.52a Neisha Crosland: Lino block print.

on and on, reproduced in different colourways, using different techniques: looking every bit as modern as the Russian avant-garde artists I'd just encountered at the George Costakis exhibition at the RA at the time.

I knew instantly that I'd made a mistake and that I should be studying textiles.

Luckily I managed to arrange a switch from graphics to textiles. One of my first textile projects at art school was to cut into a small bit of wood, 2 x 10 cm, and print with it for a whole week. I found it intriguing that so many different patterns could be created by printing one simple block / motif in different sequences. I was also intrigued by how the effectiveness of

the pattern repeat relied on the negative spaces between the printed—it was a sort of yin and yang effect. My love affair with the power of the repeat pattern had begun. And funnily enough this design has now been produced by Christopher Farr.

I then went on to do an MA at the RCA where I experimented with print techniques. I was picked up by Antony Little of Osborne & Little and invited to do a collection based on my MA show. This was a fantastic opportunity and training ground for a graduate, especially as then Osborne & Little had their wallpaper printing on the floor below the studio, so I got to learn the process.

Figure 3.52b Neisha Crosland: Drum fabric print at Christopher Farr.

Figure 3.53 Neisha Crosland: Osborne & Little *Romanga* collection poster.

REPEAT: What is it about repeating patterns within interiors that excites and inspires you?

NC: A room with its walls, floors and furniture offers a stage set for pattern. If you think about it, it is pretty audacious to line four walls of a room with wallpaper pattern—especially if you want to hang pictures on it. The repeat of a pattern has a chance to gain momentum on the flat expanse of a wall and pick up a rhythm—I like the challenge of designing for wallpapers. It is in fact the most difficult product to design, as it demands a lot of attention in getting it right. Any ugly flaws or imbalance in the repeat become obviously visible—there are no creases or seams or folds for repeat flaws to hide in. The excitement of an upholstery fabric when applied to a sofa / chair is that it transforms into a three-dimensional sculptural form—the pattern on the fabric gets a bit fractured when being cut up and sewn together. A sort of cubist effect takes hold! There is a conundrum with a rug, as on one hand it has to hold a room together but not be too distracting and it must look good from all angles and not mind having furniture covering it. A repeat pattern on a pair of curtains needs to look good when drawn and also when opened … those folds can play havoc with repeating motifs.

REPEAT: Can you explain briefly your preferred process of creating a pattern that repeats?

NC: Pattern making is not simply an act of arranging shapes into a pleasing composition. It is about making the parts function as a whole—the cog wheels need to click into the correct position in order to carry the repeat forward and strum up a rhythm—a visual tune, if you like—for me it is this tune that gives the pattern a character.

The process starts with a spark that is ignited by seeing something that inspires me. Picking up inspiration is second nature to creatives—it's just something that happens along the way. It is the easy bit. What you do with it afterwards is what counts … the ideas need processing and there is an order to this that starts with a pinboard wall space and drawing for me.

I must emphasize the importance of the close examination that drawing brings—and its inherent imperfections. I prefer an imperfect line to a digitally generated one. The imperfection of the human touch has a vulnerability that gives soul. However, I am very lucky as I have the best of two worlds—the experience of pre-digital-age art school with lots of drawing, painting and experimenting with print techniques, combined with the current digital-age speed which enables me to work on several projects at once.

I have a lot of wall space in my studio and the walls are lined with sliding metallic panels. It all starts with the chaotic pinboard which is where I throw all my bits of inspiration at, like a dartboard—a postcard from a trip to a museum, a coloured ribbon or a photo that I have printed off my phone—sometimes it might be just a written note or doodle to remind me of an idea; seemingly random things that have caught my eye. I then live with these inspirations—sometimes for months or years before any of them trigger the seed of an idea—the ideas that survive then migrate to take their place on one of the metal panels. I start sketching a layout in rough repeat at this point, giving each idea a working title—sometimes two ideas combine to become one idea and are given a double-barreled name and, like a boardgame, move to join each other on the same metal panel. When I am confident that I am on to something, I will trace it out in life-size scale; this is very important to me and must not be done on a computer screen as it would diminish the emotional contact with the design. This mapping out of the design is done in black pen or pencil, as colour would be a distraction at this point. I like to get the bones and the structure of the design right before the colouring proceeds.

Once I am happy with the tracing, I scan it and print off several drops life-size and hang them side by side on my metal panels. I stand back and look at it, appraise it and spot any ugly repeating shapes that might be there—it is often the spaces between the drawing that are the culprit. I repeat this process until I am happy.

My training at Camberwell and the Royal College of Art in the 1980s drilled into me the importance of drawing and a step-by-step process. I learnt to appreciate and respect each step from drawing to screen making to mixing dyes, etc.—as a separate adventure that eventually links everything together. This includes going into an art shop to choose paints, pencils, paper and brushes, squeezing paint tubes for the mixing of colour, the sharpening of pencils, the smell of the wood shavings as you wait for the perfect point—these experiences remain

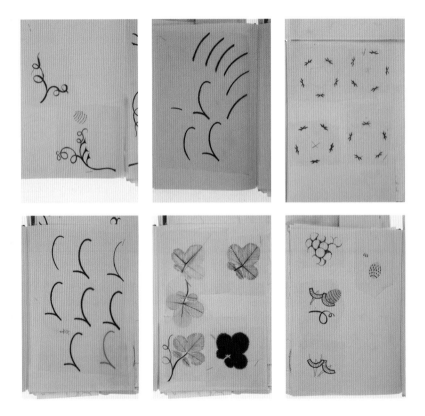

Figure 3.54 Neisha Crosland: sketchbook ideas.

equally exciting and important to me as a visit to a factory to discuss production. All are an important part of the design process, that inspire me.

REPEAT: You have designed for many different surface products. How important is the end product / surface application when it comes to design decisions for the pattern?

NC: You can't just plonk a pattern on something, you need to have a sense of the visual suitability of the pattern for the type of product that it is being applied to, as well as ask yourself what the manufacturing process will do to the look of the surface pattern.

With manufacturing possibilities come constraints that need to be considered:

— The repeat always has to work within a set of fixed dimensions whether it is the circumference of a wallpaper printing roller, the width of the paper dimensions of a tile or the limitation of number of yarn colours a loom can weave, etc.
— The pixilated effect that cut pile and loop pile have on designs for carpets and velvet fabric means that you cannot achieve very fine straight lines.
— Surface-printed wallpapers have a beautiful block print, slightly raised effect, but it also means that fine detail gets lost because they go blobby.
— All print rollers and screens have a cost implication when it comes to the number of colours you use. If you want to have many colours then digital printing is the way to go, but this can print rather flat, although there are very good textured substrates to print on.
— My handmade tiles are screen printed but any fine lines are hand painted—they have

a wonderful irregular patina which gives them their charm.
— Vinyl flooring and porcelain tile colours can look very crude and flat—also the pattern needs to incorporate a gap around the edges of the vinyl floor tile to allow for easy laying as, due to the flatness, any slightly off registration pattern will show up. This is a wonderfully inexpensive hardwearing flooring.
— A flock fabric is not so suitable for upholstery as the flock will wear off after a lot of sitting.

With colour and repeat pattern there are things to consider like:

— What happens to the design when colour is applied, as the colour on a computer or gouache-painted design will not look the same as a printed colour on cloth, etc. Have you given your customer a balance of options to suit different tastes and moods—soft, pretty / strong and dark? These are all factors that need to be considered.
— Pattern on a carpet must feel grounded. I always find it funny that one can agonize over the pattern layout or composition of a rug which often gets covered with furniture or hidden under a sofa. A carpet or rug needs to pull a room together; it must look good from all angles, from all corners of the room, so I avoid making the repeat pattern directional. The scale of the pattern and layout of the design for a rug must work within its dimension—a bit like the setting of a stone on a ring.
— A wallpaper wraps itself around a room, often commanding attention, so it is essential to get the balance of pattern,

with its repeat and perfectly pitched colouring—you do not want one colour leaping out, so the balance has got to be absolutely right to avoid this. A wallpaper has gravity to consider. You would not want apples to be dangling up to the ceiling. It would feel all upside down and unnatural.

— With tiles you need to consider how the pattern might get affected by the interruption of the grid effect of the grouting.

— Can a pattern cope with being fractured and disjointed when applied to a sofa. You might not want the elements of a huge pattern to disappear over the back of a sofa.

— Is the distortion of a geometric pattern when wrapped around a bowl shape or mug going to work / enhance the design?— in some cases, yes, in some cases, no—it depends on the pattern.

I usually have an idea of how the design should be executed but often in fact the technique will actually inspire the design. Once the design is handed over to the manufacturer there will be a back and forth with sampling / prototyping.

Figure 3.55 Neisha Crosland: Tumbleweed Epingle, pixilation.

Figure 3.56 Neisha Crosland: Fine china

Figure 3.57a Neisha Crosland: Tango fine line painting.

Figure 3.57b Neisha Crosland: Tango tile.

Each stage of the process is an adventure. You can never be too sure or fixed in your ways, as wonderful, unexpected things pop up often in the form of what can be considered a mistake. It is important to have an open-minded approach

to these unexpected turns, as this is when you make new discoveries.

REPEAT: How do you know when you've created a successful repeat pattern? What makes it successful?

NC: Basically, when I stop fussing over it—I no longer feel the urge to make more tweaks and I find myself impatient to move on to something else. It will feel settled, have a personality and a sense of joy.

The drawing should look elegant, the repeat well-balanced with a perfect sense of proportion and scale.

REPEAT: Which designer of patterns inspires you?

NC: Early humankind—today we have so many easily accessible visual references—to feed our work. I am in awe of early humankind's pattern making, as they did not have anything to plagiarize or influence them—they just had what they

Figure 3.58 Neisha Crosland: Triangles, Lines, Spokes.

Figure 3.59a Neisha Crosland: Zebra, hand painting.

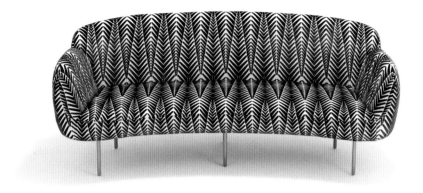

Figure 3.59b Neisha Crosland: Zebra fabric, silver blue, on Sé Collections sofa.

saw in front of them. The Neolithic and early Paleo Age has handed down to us a repertoire of wonderful geometric patterns etched on to Ice Age mammoth teeth, cave walls, pottery, woven fabrics—all of which are still relevant today.

Ottoman Empire—the fifteenth/sixteenth-century Ottoman Empire dots and crescents.

Cintamani and tulip designs were a huge inspiration to me—the bold, strong and simple and beautiful and utterly modern-looking.

Japanese—early kimonos, fourteenth- to seventeenth-century, for their seemingly effortless ability to depict a flower on a kimono. Japanese designers managed to express everything about that flower with the minimum of brush strokes and with great subtlety of colour. I am intrigued by the way they laid out a pattern across a kimono, trailing it off over the sleeves in a care-free manner, as if it was the most natural thing in the world. The strength of the composition

matched by the lyricism of the brush stroke. The boldness and economy of line—dynamic, but beautiful too. I am impressed again by the contrast of technical virtuosity and the mixing and layering of different techniques—always carried out with respect for the balance of the whole. They maintain a sense of meditation and spirituality.

Bizarre silks of the eighteenth century—namely, James Leman and Marie Garthwaite for their fantastical woven silks, aptly named bizarre silks. The fluidity of their drawing of fantastical shapes and outlandish plant forms that they manage to tether, done into clever seamless repeats. For their sense of mad colour combinations—bubble-gum pinks, lime greens and tangerine oranges …

Indienne block prints and hand-painted fabrics of the seventeenth century … the draw-ing and interpretation of flora and fauna, let alone the clever work of the artisans with dyes and dying techniques.

Raoul Duffy textile designs—for their joyfulness and lyrical ease.

Barron and Larcher—for the effect of their clever simple repeating motifs.

Leon Bakst / Natalia Goncharova —for their full of vitality and energetic patterns for Diaghilev's ballets.

Many designers behind so many wonderful designs are anonymous and even today many sell designs to great fabric / fashion houses without recognition.

REPEAT: What have you learnt in your career that has helped you be a better pattern designer?

NC:

- The experience of working with many different surfaces and products and in so many different techniques with different manufacturers has shown me how pattern can transform itself according to how it is applied.
- The importance of colour to change the mood of a design. The value of sensitivity and respect for material—a pattern for silk velvet might not work for vinyl flooring.
- The importance of a gestation period—a time to contemplate my work.
- That it is important to recognize where ideas come from, as we can take for granted the wonderful sources of inspiration that have been handed down through the ages. A good design will have a sense of déjà vu with a fresh point of view and therefore an emotional appeal. The customer can sense when real thought

and care have gone into a design and they want to be surprised but not alienated.

REPEAT: Please select one of your most successful repeating designs for interiors and talk us through how you developed the design.

NC: Hollywood Grape—

It was my first trip to India. I was in the middle of the Delhi Craft Museum, and the museum was about to close. I was desperate to see as much as possible of the textiles, so my friend Elana Dickson kept the museum guards distracted by chatting to them, allowing me to scoot round, desperately trying to feast my eyes on as much as possible. I must have got halfway through when I spotted a most intriguing design of grapes and flowers in bubble-gum pink, saffron yellow, violet, and moss and lime green. It did not have a date or provenance, but later Dr Ruchira Ghosh told me that it was from nineteenth-century Kashmir.

The technique used is called *kani*. There are three main types of *kani* shawl—*mughal*, *sikh* and *dogra*—and the interesting thing about this textile was that it did not seem to fall comfortably into any of these three categories. There seemed even to be some European influence in the design. Luckily I had just enough time to snap it with my camera before Elana's conversation with the guards ran out of steam and we were politely chucked out.

When I got back to the studio in London I pinned the photo to the wall. I knew it would one day inspire a design, but it took a while. The bright bubble-gum pinks, violets, saffron and lime colours easily poured themselves into scarf designs but what I really wanted to do was something with those grapes.

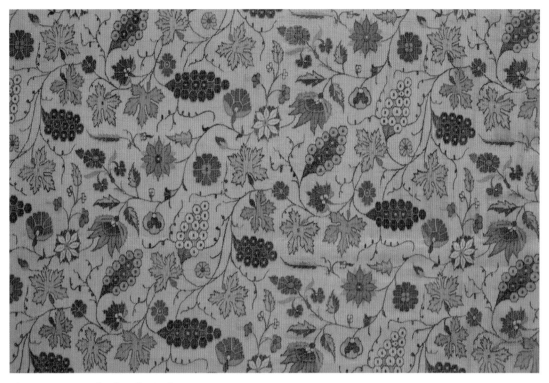

Figure 3.60 Kani shawl, Delhi Craft Museum.

On starting a new design I always ask myself, *Why am I bothering? What is it that I think is interesting about this idea? Is it worth pursuing?* So in the case of this Kashmir *kani* textile I asked myself, *Why not just leave the design as a snapshot on the wall to admire?* I did not really know the answer. I felt like a copycat, a terrible plagiarizer, but I felt curiously compelled. I started tracing the outline of the design to get to know it, a bit like caressing a new lover for the first time without knowing whether there is a relationship in store for us.

I extract and modify the elements that I like. I put them into a single unit to create the *tile repeat* (this is called a *tile* in surface pattern design). I enlarge it on the photocopier to the size I remember it being in real life. I stick about ten tiles together and then trace it on to tracing paper. But it loses all that was beautiful about the original, and I do not know what to do next. However, I still feel that an idea is lurking. In this situation, my mantra is always do what the Russian avant-garde artists did and what the Japanese did: reduce the design to its bare minimum. *Minimum line for maximum impact*, I keep repeating to myself.

I stare over my drawing board across the gardens and backyards of the houses backing on to my studio. I see the windows of kitchens and bathrooms and the drainpipes climbing their way up the brickwork. I begin to draw them and realize that a stepping repeat is emerging on my drawing board. This ubiquitous part of the urban landscape is giving me the solution for the structure of my design. The grapes migrate, they cluster and alight like a flock of sparrows on a washing line, and the pattern and repeat reveal themselves. The pattern reaches over the edge of the board and on and on. It has no edges and the middle is everywhere.

At the same time, Radio 4 is in the middle of a programme on the excesses of Hollywood and its glamour in the 1940s. I realize that the geometric hexagonal shape of the grapes looks very deco to me and very out-of-keeping with the rest of the florid and otherwise naturalistic nature of the fabric. Also I realize grapes are meant to be round, whereas my clusters of grapes look like old threepenny bits. Looking back, I realize that this odd juxtaposition was the very thing that had first drawn my attention in the museum.

It so happened that, at the time, we were planting an espaliered *Parrotia persica* against our garden wall, so it is no wonder that I ended up laying this deco grape design out across my paper like a well-behaved espalier tree. I pruned back all the unnecessary foliage and flowers. I had now left the Delhi Craft Museum behind and invented a completely new design. With Hollywood glamour in my mind and inspired by deco mirrors, interiors, white leather sofas and the spirit of Gloria Swanson, I even banished the vivid colour spectrum.

Colour has enormous power. As with a chameleon, it can completely change the mood of a design. On my desk was the latest copy of the magazine *World of Interiors*. It featured Lenny Kravitz's house, full of white leather and silver metals, and this settled me on the idea of printing the design on silver and gold metal foil paper. I called the design Hollywood Grape.

Figure 3.61 Neisha Crosland: Hollywood Grape, design in progress.

Figure 3.62 Neisha Crosland: Hollywood Grape, design in progress.

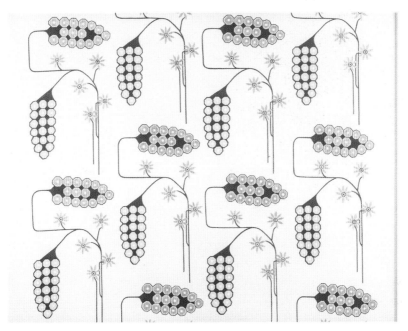

Figure 3.63 Neisha Crosland: Hollywood Grape, hand-painting.

Figure 3.64 Neisha Crosland: Hollywood Grape fabric on the Siamese Sofa by India Mahdavi.

DESIGNER INTERVIEW

Timorous Beasties

Noted for surreal and provocative textiles and wallpapers, the design studio Timorous Beasties was founded in Glasgow in 1990 by Alistair McAuley and Paul Simmons, who met while studying textile design at Glasgow School of Art. The name 'Timorous Beasties' is taken from the poem 'To a Mouse' by Scotland's much celebrated poet, Robert Burns.

Refusing to follow trends, Timorous Beasties' work embodies a unique mastery of diverse pattern, ranging from design that echoes a golden age of copperplate engraving, to examples of a distinctly edgy nature. Timorous Beasties' work could be seen as a wayward take on the often 'twee' world of textiles, with heavily illustrative insects, 'triffid'-like plants, birds and other animals. They are also known for their contemporary take on the *'toile de Jouy'* fabrics of Napoleonic France. The studio fully engages in a

Figure 3.66 Timorous Beasties: Alistair McAuley and Paul Simmons.

Figure 3.65 Timorous Beasties: Fruit Looters wallpaper.

design discourse with textiles history by lending an aesthetic evolution to time-honoured motifs.

REPEAT: How did you both become designers of pattern? What training did you undertake? Did you always know this is what you wanted to do?

TB (Paul): I always knew I wanted to do art because it was the one thing I was good at. Once at art school it became a process of elimination. I wasn't good at three-dimensional work, so that ruled out product design, sculpture, ceramics and jewellery. Many of our contemporaries were into fine art, but in a conceptual and performance art way, and I knew I didn't have the dedication for that. Graphic design and illustration seemed too prosaic at the time, which just left me with textiles.

In textile design there were three possible specializations: knit, weave and print. It was print that appealed most, because with printed textiles, you can use images, draw, paint, and learn how to make a physical product; it all seemed to fit with what I was about. After Glasgow School of Art I went on to study at the Royal College.

REPEAT: Was it always interiors you wanted to design for, rather than for fashion? Why?

TB (Paul): I was always more interested in interiors than in fashion. There seemed to be more longevity in patterns made for interiors. They're grander and larger in scale. Also, the designers of furnishing patterns seemed more recognized and better known (Josef Frank, Barbara Brown, William Morris). In the fashion world a textile designer is rarely credited, and a lot of the patterned designs are created to keep up with

Figure 3.67 Timorous Beasties: Indie Wood Black wallpaper.

trends, and with no synchronicity between process and the final product.

REPEAT: Can you explain briefly your preferred process of creating a pattern that repeats?

TB (Paul): Inspiration can come from anything and everything. However, we do often use classic patterns as a reference point. The pattern often starts with a pen and ink drawing, then the drawing is cut in half, and the top half is placed at the bottom, and the bottom half is swapped round vice versa to the top, then the rest of the pattern is drawn in-between the gap between the top and bottom. This gives you the vertical repeat. Currently the drawings are still created by hand, but scanned into the computer, where it's much easier these days to see how the pattern works for scale, structure and composition.

REPEAT: What role does digital design software play in your design process?

TB (Paul): Computers and digital technologies will never make anyone 'more creative', but they are great for working out repeats, colouring designs, and simply for storing all one's artwork. It's rather like comparing letter writing to email:

the content is still the same, but it's all made easier with technology.

REPEAT: You have created designs for a wide number of interiors surfaces, including carpets and wallpapers as well as upholstery. How does each surface / product shape your design thinking?

TB (Paul): It is always important to know about how something is going to be made in order to design for it—whether it's digital, hand print, lace, jacquard, carpet, textiles or wallcoverings—design for process is essential.

REPEAT: What makes a successful repeat pattern?

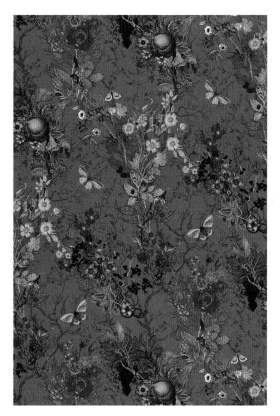

Figure 3.68 Timorous Beasties: Bloomsbury Garden.

Figure 3.69 Timorous Beasties: Merian Palm, wallpaper.

Figure 3.70a Timorous Beasties: Devil Damask lace, detail.

Figure 3.70b Timorous Beasties: Devil Damask lace.

TB (Paul): Essentially a repeat pattern has to flow, and hide the join of the repeat. Certain proportions and compositions (as with the golden triangle in painting) can apply, but it depends on what surface the pattern is going on, and on its purpose.

REPEAT: You have referenced historical pattern design in past projects—which era or designer of patterns continues to inspire you, and why?

TB (Paul): The eighteenth-century French toile de Jouy fabrics have always been a source of inspiration. The imagery in the toiles from that era was often dark and macabre, the

Figure 3.70c Timorous Beasties: Devil Damask Olive.

Figure 3.71 Timorous Beasties: Golden Oriole fabric.

patterns often depicting moral tales or actual historical events. They were beautifully, finely printed with copper plates usually in red or blue on to linen, with extraordinary detail that even the best digital printer could never match. One of our favourite toile designs is 'Peacock Amongst the Ruins' in the V&A collection. It's a breathtaking example of the printed image. We used its name to title an exhibition we had at the DCA [Dundee Contemporary Arts] in 2007. We have also made our own idiosyncratic version of the toiles, and produced patterns depicting Glasgow, London, Edinburgh and New York.

REPEAT: How have your design processes changed over your careers so far, and what are the challenges of adapting?

Figure 3.72 Timorous Beasties: Glasgow Toile.

TB (Paul): We have always embraced new processes and technologies rather than being Luddite about them (ironically, the Luddites were the people who smashed up weaving looms in the early nineteenth century!). Digital print technologies have brought new ways of printing that would never have been possible decades ago. In recent years, the digital process was used to make prototypes, but now the prototype has become the final product. The number of colours available and the scale of repeats is something that is utterly new. Sometimes we mix both digital and hand print in a high-tech-meets-low-tech way. Some wallpapers we hand print on top of a digital print. All the processes are very important to us. I think the challenge is to always try and push the boundaries, and use the best qualities of those processes to their greatest advantage. After all, Darwinism is about the survival of the most adaptable rather than the survival of the fittest, is it not? To quote Darwin himself: *It is not the strongest of the species that survives, nor the most intelligent; it is the one most adaptable to change.*

Figure 3.73 Timorous Beasties: Bloody Empire wallpaper.

Figure 3.74 Timorous Beasties: screen printing wallpaper.

Figure 3.75 Timorous Beasties: Storm Blotch.

REPEAT: What advice can you share to inspire new designers of pattern for interiors?

TB (Ali): Like everyone, we like to experiment, challenge and try not to be too commercial. We are aware of our niche position which gives us the freedom to try new ideas, the results of which can reveal their value in different ways. We design with the final product in mind; each can require a different handling and they don't always cross over, sometimes a pattern works as a wallcovering but not as a fabric, and so on. Pattern adds another layer of detail and interest to a space—it can direct the mood, influence the use and reflect aspirations. Being aware of these can help inspire a different approach and response to a brief. In such a competitive and subjective market, we have found inspiration in the cracks and the broken bits of what would be considered traditional surface decoration. We love the history of pattern and value the craft and labour that is involved in creating for interiors.

REPEAT: Please select one of your most successful repeating designs for interiors and talk us through how you developed the design. What were the considerations and changes that occurred in the process of designing it?

TB (Ali): Omni Drips Repeating Wallpaper / Fabric and Thunder Blotch.

The design was developed by combining a traditionally structured damask pattern with a random mark-making process. Rather than precisely placing colour within the pattern, the areas were redefined by carefully distributing the bleeds and splashes to allude to a traditional damask. While the pattern is a strong structured repeat, the distance between the repeats on the wallcovering can be varied specifically for the elevation, to make the paper more suited to the height of the wall. This is really only possible because of the digital process, but it does give a tailored end result. For Thunder Blotch the same pattern is printed railroad, to make upholstery much easier, specifically for the backs of sofas. No seams, no waste.

Figure 3.76 Timorous Beasties: Omni Drips.

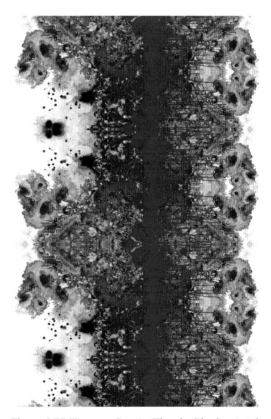

Figure 3.77 Timorous Beasties: Thunder Blotch, printed 'railroad'.

Figure 3.78 Galbraith & Paul: In the studio.

DESIGNER INTERVIEW
Galbraith & Paul

G albraith & Paul is a studio-based business founded in the US city of Philadelphia in 1986 by Liz Galbraith and Ephi Paul. All of their designs are created by Liz and produced in their studio, where a talented staff of artists and artisans work together. The studio originally specialized in traditional Japanese hand paper making, and created a line of lighting with patterned translucent paper lampshades that sold throughout the United States. In 1996, Liz began experimenting with hand block printing and fell in love with the directness and simplicity of the process. The studio changed its focus entirely in 2000 to hand blocking fabric for yardage and pillows, innovating the ancient craft with Liz's painterly approach to the surface. In 2013, a line of wallpaper was added to their collection using digital technology to translate the hand block printed artwork on to the wall. Over their history, Liz has designed more than 125 original patterns, all made in their Philadelphia studio and seen throughout the world.

REPEAT: How did you become a designer of pattern?

LG: My love of pattern, process and craft came from my mother. I am the youngest of six, born to a loving mother and homemaker who was also a frustrated artist and entrepreneur. When she decided she wanted to make something, she went all in, travelled to the source and mastered it. One example is when she wanted to learn how to knit Aran sweaters … so we flew from Chicago to Ireland, took a boat to the Isle of Aran, where she bought yarn and studied the sweater patterns. Once home she knitted and reknitted the same sweater until she got it just the way she wanted it. I was 12 then and am now 59, and I still have and wear the first Aran sweater she knitted for herself after that trip.

I have always loved textiles and was trained as a painter. When I discovered block printing it felt like the perfect mix between craft and art. My love of patterns came out of my love of block printing and my pattern designs come out of this process. The line quality of the blocks and ability to flip them and play with them on the table is an important part of my pattern development.

Figure 3.79 Galbraith & Paul: Seville Medallion design.

Figure 3.80 Galbraith & Paul: printing Lotus.

REPEAT: What is it about repeating patterns that excites you?

LG: Hand block printing requires a registration system to print in repeat. Our repeat system is based on an 18 x 17.5-inch grid. I love the challenge of working with these limits, to create a variety of scales within our system, and to work with positive and negative space. The grid presents a multitude of ways to create a repeat. Some of our patterns are simple with a small repeat, and others are double-long with a half-drop down the centre, and printed with multiple blocks. Some patterns hide their repeats, while others highlight the grid and celebrate the fact that it's been hand block printed. The possibilities seem endless and I like the confines of this format.

REPEAT: Can you explain briefly your preferred process of creating a pattern that repeats? You utilize traditional methods to print the fabric—how does this influence your design process?

LG: I do all of the design work for our company and our collection is very small and edited. I usually have a few designs that I am working on at the same time, and these are often based on things I think are missing from our collection. Inspiration usually comes from

Figure 3.81 Galbraith & Paul: Valerian.

Figure 3.82 Galbraith & Paul: Mother Nature.

my travels, the garden and fashion and many times a personal need … like we need curtains for our library. The first step of my process usually involves magic markers, the copying machine, tape and scissors. If I decide I want to pursue the idea further, I will make a block and begin experimenting on the print table. Process is very important to me and in our studio. We mix all of our own paints and I like to play with the transparency and opacity as another element in the design. When we block print, we first roll the paint on to the blocks and that is another design consideration. We use different-sized rollers and one shape might have two different colours rolled on to it in different thicknesses. The effect is very painterly. I really am unlike most textile designers in my process because I design in the process of making.

REPEAT: How important is the end product / application when it comes to design decisions?

LG: The end product is very important to me. That is why we design our own patterns, make our own blocks, mix our own paint, and then print the fabric in our studio. I want my designs to feel both timeless and original and to be at home in many different environments. We print on natural grounds and the hand and feel of my work are very important.

Figure 3.83 Galbraith & Paul: the printing block.

Figure 3.84 Galbraith & Paul: Sumi wallpaper.

REPEAT: Which designer of patterns inspires you?

LG: Biggest design influences: Marimekko for the boldness of scale and the use of colour; Fortuny for the sense of the process and the hand; William Morris for the studio workshop tradition.

REPEAT: What advice can you share to inspire new designers of pattern for interiors?

LG: I think it's important to develop your own personal point of view. By this I mean looking at a lot of different things and educating your-self in the history of textiles, art, interior design and architecture. The more you look at the more you will begin to develop your own personal aesthetic and taste. That will be what sets you apart and makes your work original. I also think it's really nice if you can have time for your designs to incubate. I know this is very difficult in the design world because you are often on deadlines but it is nice when you can have the time to step back and get some distance from a design so you can look at it with fresh eyes. I like to keep a physical scrapbook of clippings of rooms, art, fashion and gardens … really just things I like and feel inspired by. This process of gathering images will also help you hone your own point of view.

Figure 3.85 Galbraith & Paul: Sakura Blossom.

REPEAT: Please select one of your most successful repeating designs for interiors and talk us through how you developed the design, step by step. What were the considerations and changes that occurred in the process of designing it?

LG: I like it when my ideas come out of my travels. In designing the Koi Pond, I was inspired by a picture I took years ago of a koi pond in Puerto Rico and a piece of antique seaweed I bought at Portobello Market in London. I wanted to make a wallpaper with fish and decided to combine these two ideas. I drew the seaweed, simplified it, and cut a block from it. I then cut out a variety of fish shapes and began to play with these blocks on the table, experimenting with different types of markings on the fish.

Figure 3.86 Galbraith & Paul: sampling Koi Pond.

I wanted the fish to feel like they were moving and wanted the process to reflect this, so I used my fingers to stroke gestures on to the fish and added markings with different colours. The movement of the fish became important and also I wanted them to feel playful because at one point in the design they felt a little menacing and shark-like. There are two types of fish and I wanted them each to be swimming in different patterns. The small fish became a single accent colour which flowed throughout the pattern and the larger fish became more about the marking on them. With the seaweed I rolled in a few tones of the same colour on to it and had the edges fade away. The seaweed became the organizing structure for the fish to flow around. Once the pattern was formed I began working on the colourways, thinking both of unusual combinations and some standard easy-to-use classic combinations. I often try to envision rooms for the papers and fabrics and sometimes, once the pattern is finished, I will pick some rooms to design colourways for. Pattern making is a process and my favourite patterns are ones that evolve and change from the original idea. I am lucky to have the luxury of time in my design process, while many young designers are under pressure to meet deadlines.

Figure 3.87 Galbraith & Paul: Koi Pond, print development.

Figure 3.88 Galbraith & Paul: Koi Pond wallpaper.

Figure 3.89 Deborah Bowness: Painted Wall in Moscow wallpaper.

DESIGNER INTERVIEW

Deborah Bowness

Deborah Bowness has created a path of her own in printed wallpaper design. Shaped by her love of pattern, she developed her unique contemporary take on trompe l'oeil wallpapers during her time at the Royal College of Art, London, combining monochrome photographic imagery with hand-printed colour in bespoke drops. Her graduate collection *Hooks and Frocks* brought together interior accessories and garments as printed interior surface decoration for wallpaper. She has continued to push her conceptual understanding of designing pattern for an interior environment for over two decades, taking her view of the world to a global audience through a combination of craft practice and digital technology.

Combining her passion for photography and hand silkscreen printing, her papers are one-off pieces, at times customizable, as feature statements for both domestic and commercial spaces. Deborah broke with traditional manufacturing

Figure 3.90 Deborah Bowness: studio portrait.

Figure 3.91 Deborah Bowness: Hooks and Frocks wallpaper.

Figure 3.92 Deborah Bowness: in the studio.

expectations as well as commercial limitations, working with brands to create bespoke commissions for retail spaces and hospitality environments as well as cultural and heritage projects. Bowness has an international client list, including Paul Smith, Philip Starck, Polydor, the Victoria and Albert Museum, Lecroix and Selfridges. She has exhibited widely and was awarded the 2000 Peugeot Design Award and the Homes and Gardens award in 2016.

REPEAT: How did you become a designer of pattern?

DB: Pattern appealed to me from an early age. I was obsessed with Laura Ashley wallpapers and Liberty floral prints. I also loved the brightly patterned works of the potters Clarice Cliff and Susie Cooper, specifically the repetition of mass production with slight variations due to the hand-painted application of the pattern. It was not surprising when I specialized in textiles on my foundation course and went on to do a surface

Figure 3.93 Deborah Bowness: print room screens.

Figure 3.94 Deborah Bowness: set up for screen printing.

pattern and textile degree. I feel free when lost in composition of shape, image and colour.

REPEAT: Can you explain briefly how you work with pattern and your relationship with repeating imagery?

DB: My ideas start on the street where I spend time with my camera, capturing the things that catch my eye through photography. I then create pattern from these photographic images of everyday objects, the places we inhabit and spaces around us. I use collage and photomontage to make and arrange miniature versions of my designs. The resulting enlarged design is made up of multiples which create the illusion of pattern rather than conventional repeating patterns. There is no pattern match in my designs—my wallpapers can be hung as they come off the roll.

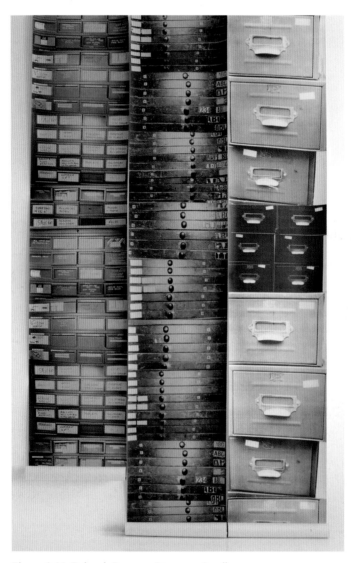

Figure 3.95 Deborah Bowness: Drawers x 3 wallpaper.

REPEAT: Is the repeating pattern important as a design element or as a way of manufacturing wallpaper in your practice, or maybe both?

DB: Repeating pattern is a by-product, I manufacture and design wallpaper to make my art useful / functional. Wallpaper provides a medium to carry my work into homes and spaces. The majority of my wallpapers do not repeat along the length—it is in the hanging that the client is able to create their own unique pattern across the width of the wall. This is achieved by the building up of multiple imagery which produces repetition.

REPEAT: How important is the end product / application when it comes to design decisions?

DB: Mine is an intuitive, unconscious design process, starting with the initial photography. I see and capture the correct scale of detail to make the required visual statement for the intended design outcome. My use of colour is usually subtle; I only add what is needed to enhance the three-dimensional quality of my prints. I believe that all my wallpapers are site-specific. They are created to exist on a wall in an unknown place. Every install is different and so there become multiple ways to hang my wallpapers. For me it is important to take into consideration the papered wall as my end product.

REPEAT: What factors do you believe make a successful repeat pattern?

Figure 3.96 Deborah Bowness: Glassware wallpaper.

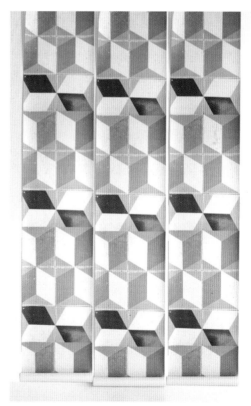

Figure 3.97 Deborah Bowness: Tiles wallpaper.

DB: The illusion and perception of a pattern repeat.

REPEAT: Which designer of patterns inspires you?

DB: I am inspired by Henri Matisse's cut-outs. He used cut-out coloured paper shapes to make patterned artworks.

REPEAT: What advice can you share to inspire new designers of pattern for interiors and wallpaper specifically?

DB: There are no limits. If you strive to do things differently and invent your own methods, you are able to sidestep the limitations of convention. By doing this I created my own unique path to creating wallpapers that repeat in very unconventional ways.

REPEAT: How did the bookshelf wallpaper come about?

DB: The 'Genuine Fake Bookshelf' is a remake of the classic fake bookshelf wallpaper. It was

Figure 3.98a Deborah Bowness: Genuine Fake Bookshelf, detail.

Figure 3.98b Deborah Bowness: Genuine Fake Bookshelf, aligned shelves.

designed using actual developed, hand-stuck, black and white photographs to create photomontage images of bookshelves, assembled to create the illusion of a floor-to-ceiling library. The images of the books naturally dictate the design without much interference from me. I can only really make small changes to a design—the designs either work or don't work, they flow and look real / right or they don't. Only after its conception did I consider that the wallpaper drops could be hung in two different ways: randomly to create an ad hoc wall of books, or uniformly by lining up the shelves to create an orderly pattern which repeats horizontally across the wall.

Figure 3.99 Deborah Bowness: Genuine Fake Bookshelf wallpaper.

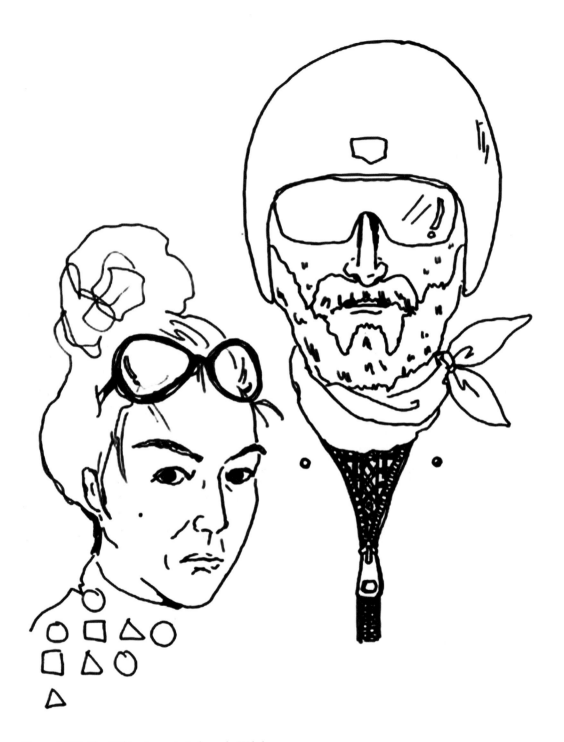

Figure 3.100 Eley Kishimoto: portrait, drawn by Wakako.

DESIGNER INTERVIEW

Eley Kishimoto

iving by the maxim 'print the world', Eley Kishimoto have always strived to create work that is executed simply, clear in intention, exhibiting a unique creative flair, and that rejects passing trends and fads.

From a partnership forged in the early 1990s, Eley Kishimoto quickly gained a reputation for incisive and intelligent print design, with their work being displayed on the catwalks of the world through work with Louis Vuitton, Marc Jacobs, Alexander McQueen, Alber Elbaz and Jil Sander, to name but a few.

In the mid-90s the partnership moved into the fashion world with the launch of their first womenswear collection; this proved to be such a success that the company has produced collections ever since.

Although initially earned as a result of these vibrant fashion collections, the company's renown has always been very much associated with their freedom to decorate anything and everything. It is this print design aesthetic that is key to their works' identity. Thus, following hot on the hemline of these collections, came a steady stream of ever more varied design products. Wallpapers, furniture, furnishing fabrics, glassware and crockery led on to more industrial-based design work in the automotive, architectural and electronics worlds, while also working with individual artists and galleries. The company sees each new design challenge as a platform from which to communicate with a wider, more varied audience.

Past collaborative works with BMW motorbikes, Vans, Volkswagen, Eastpak, Duvel, Incase, WESC, Local Motors, Tatras, Rambold, Conran, Almacantar, MICA, Squire, 6a, Studio Weave and Brixton, amongst others, have incorporated new initiatives as well as archive prints such as the signature Flash print. These projects represent a desire to constantly reinvigorate and evolve the design aesthetic of the company.

REPEAT: How did you become pattern designers and establish Eley Kishimoto?

EK (Wakako): Love for soulful beauty with hidden maths within.

REPEAT: What is it about repeating patterns that excites you both?

Figure 3.101 Eley Kishimoto: Bunny Dance design.

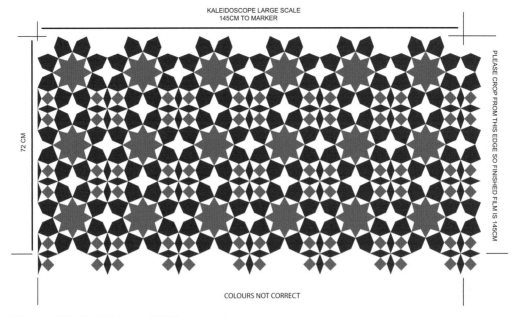

KALEIDOSCOPE LARGE SCALE
145CM TO MARKER

72 CM

PLEASE CROP FROM THIS EDGE SO FINISHED FILM IS 145CM

COLOURS NOT CORRECT

Figure 3.102 Eley Kishimoto: Kaleidoscope design.

EK (Wakako): The fact that different repetitions provide the foundation and structures for different patterns. They could be blunt or subtle, small or big, but once you create one repeating module, it can spread to infinity; nothing is too big to cover in your prints.

REPEAT: Can you explain briefly your preferred process of creating a pattern that repeats?

EK (Wakako): I decide the general dynamic and movement of the pattern, then pencil a rough sketch / draft on paper with hand-drawn rectangles and some grid lines, checking the repeat by folding / rolling the paper. I use this draft as a template for the final artwork, working on computer unless hand-painted final artwork is required, but that's very rare these days.

Figure 3.103 Eley Kishimoto: Diamond Cascade design.

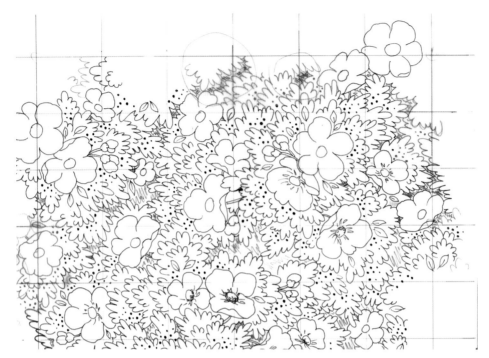

Figure 3.104 Eley Kishimoto: BA BA BLOOM CARTOON separation artwork.

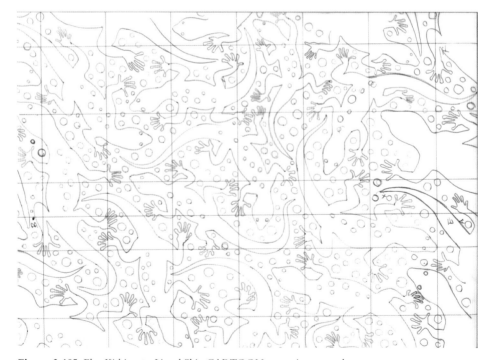

Figure 3.105 Eley Kishimoto: Lizard Skin CARTOON separation artwork.

Figure 3.106 Eley Kishimoto: Poison Garden, digital print.

REPEAT: You have designed patterns for many fashion and interiors applications—how do you adapt the design process for the different contexts?

EK (Wakako): I don't change the design process for different applications necessarily—mood, story, impact are important elements to consider for any context. Sometimes, budget or techniques can restrict some aspect of designs but that is often a fun challenge to work with.

REPEAT: What is your relationship with technology in designing and printing pattern? How has it evolved and has that changed your creative process?

EK (Wakako): It is a useful tool and makes certain tasks within my process quicker and effective. But I still start my initial process by sketching, drawing manually. I can be more natural, focused and committed when working with pencil and paper, as there are no possible other options

Figure 3.107 Eley Kishimoto: Brocade wallpaper for house at Hautefage, Studio Maclean.

luring you to change your mind, or zooming in and out to make you lose the sense of real scales and proportions. I create final artworks digitally but I am always mindful not to lose the slight off-ness that the original sketches have.

Working digitally is much more economical than creating artworks manually since you don't need all the specialist art materials, but I sort of miss my visits to art shops to get all the beautiful things with my excuse, 'need for work'!

REPEAT: Which designer(s) of patterns inspires you? (historic / contemporary)

EK (Wakako): Many designs are inspiring, but I cannot name anyone specific. I am too open and frivolous with what I like.

REPEAT: What advice can you share to inspire new designers of pattern for interiors?

EK (Wakako): Stay curious and interested. Value originality.

Figure 3.108 Eley Kishimoto: Shapes, screen-printed ply for house at Cannes, Studio Maclean.

REPEAT: In working together, how do you collaborate in the process of pattern designing? Do you have clear roles or share the process?

EK: Wakako is the Creative Director, generating concepts, narrative, artwork and all pattern design.

Mark as Director shapes all business and management development of Eley Kishimoto, coordinating the diverse range of productions / consultation and industry-collaborative projects.

REPEAT: Flash is one of your most recognizable and successful repeating designs across products and surfaces. Can you talk us through how you developed the design and how it has continued to work for the brand?

EK (Mark): Flash started with idle doodling on a corner of a page in a sketchbook. Flash is a pattern designed in 2000 and was included in the printed textiles offered to the S/S 2001 EK fashion collection *Reunion*. The following season we launched wallpapers and alternative

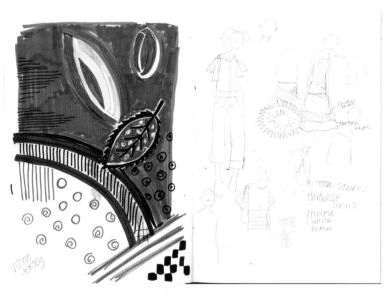

Figure 3.109 Eley Kishimoto: Wakako sketchbook.

Figure 3.110 Eley Kishimoto: Wakako sketchbook.

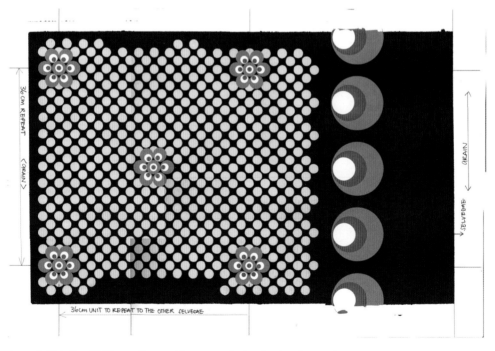

Figure 3.111 Eley Kishimoto: Eastern Moon gouache hand-painted artwork.

Figure 3.112 Eley Kishimoto: Flash SS01.

collaborations utilizing this particular pattern, and through ongoing various requests with partners and productions it has stood out as our icon.

Obviously it has become a bit of an obsession. Originally developing from the idea of taking something out of the fashion cycle for which it was designed (S/S 01) to see if we could create something within, or rather, from fashion which would have a greater longevity and versatility. A photograph taken for the look book with the model in Flash garment against a Flash fabric wall was the first step aesthetically: the girl was engulfed by Flash as it jumped from garment to wall. Wallpapers were then produced, acknowledging the seasonless quality of the print; quick on its heels came the popular Flash Converse range.

Figure 3.113 Eley Kishimoto: Flash Invitation poster, 2000.

From this starting point it has almost taken on a viral identity. Is it too much all the time, everywhere? Yes, sometimes—however, I do want certain products and friendships to exist in my life, and through the currency of Flash I have had the opportunity to make these dreams real.

As it gained its own momentum and collaborations with varying partners were introduced, Flash, having already jumped out of the fashion frame, now seemed to be the print of choice for many reasons. A multi-directional small repeat, all over a one-colour unisex print, was a very easy file to send around the world.

The kineticism evident in the print's optical movement soon became real when one started to see other Flash items in the world. The moment of frisson of Flash passing Flash is something quite unique, as we have intentionally limited the product and have only worked with partners or friends that understand this. This fleeting moment instantly unites people who do not know each other, based simply upon a surface pattern.

Figure 3.114 Eley Kishimoto: Flash Yukata and Obi Kimono Breath.

Figure 3.115 Eley Kishimoto: Going Green: Flash G-Wiz electric car, 2003.

CONCLUSION

This book brings together printed pattern in recent international history with examples from contemporary design practices to highlight how pattern has and remains a mainstay in our interior spaces. We have seen how key themes such as florals and geometrics have been shaped by the time in which they were designed but also provide a bridge to what follows. Whether it be the need for something reassuringly connected to the past, such as damask or neoclassical toile, or the challenge of creating something forward-looking, such as Art Nouveau and Modernist motifs, we see connections and relationships that designers of today explore and utilize.

Design and manufacturing methods have evolved significantly over the last 200 years, with today's digital technology enabling quick design alterations and fast production of textiles and wallpapers. A strong design stands the test of time; it provides joy and value through its design consideration, visual balance, beautiful motifs, eye-catching rhythm, and sense of colour. There is not one pattern equation a designer relies on for design success. For some, an elegantly beautiful hand-painted motif; for another, a digitally generated and colour-saturated extravaganza. A designer unites elements and ingredients to balance and resolve their own creative identity through unique patterns.

This book explores an evolution of commercially available surface designs for interiors through stylistic developments, and relationships to social and market pressures, as well as manufacturing capabilities. With this awareness, we can learn to identify our individual relationship with pattern, applying successful elements in our own design thinking. Postmodernist rule-breaking and the advent of digital software have liberated a previous formality in our pattern generation. The contemporary offer of bespoke artwork and unique finishing processes, as well as consumers playing a role in the curation of patterns on walls and surfaces, provides a glimpse into the future of patterns in our interior spaces.

We are at an exciting junction of pattern product strategy and offer a reconnection with traditional craft production in a slow-design ethos, and the emergence of digital screens as ever-changing surfaces for pattern in our living, working, education and healthcare environments. There is also the fast-developing potential of the metaverse, offering new digital contexts, including interiors, for pattern to feature in entirely virtual domains. There is space for well-considered pattern in whatever form it arrives. The designers of the future will no doubt be responding to the past while creating something new.

Figure 4.1 *Pattern Evolution* by Kate Farley is a work in progress drawing project exploring design elements that morph within and across formal pattern structures.

INDEX

Entries in bold refer to images and entries in parentheses refer to captions.

ACKNOWLEDGEMENTS

This project wouldn't be here without the belief, support and hard work from team Bloomsbury. A huge thanks to my publisher, Georgia Kennedy, for getting us up and running so many years ago and always finding time to answer questions big and small. Immeasurable thanks to my editor, Faith Marsland, for your ongoing patience and understanding as the author was once again hospitalised and as we navigate a global pandemic – your guiding hand and reassuring support delivered this book. Thank you to Deborah Maloney and the team at Integra for tolerating final final final edits, and for making this book look so good.

I am indebted to my dear husband Stuart for putting up with me and the book. From image hunter, proofreader, counsellor and advocate, I really couldn't have done this without you … and to E and A, thanks for suffering with me having my head elsewhere too often, and for sharing in my excitement as image permissions were granted – see, I told you I'd acknowledge you! A huge thanks to Lise for constant support from the sidelines, for sharing the love of all things design, and for believing this was achievable.

A heartfelt thanks to Jill & Grainne and Paul and Julie, for training me in drawing and pattern design from the very start and instilling in me a creative and enquiring design process. Thank you for your ongoing encouragement and support as I tread my own path in textile design education.

Thank you to Zoe Hillyard, dear friend and fellow academic, for always being there with moral support, wise words and belief that years of conversations about teaching textile design could and should one day lead to the writing of this book. Still an absurd thought!

Thank you to Will Crisp for reading an early draft of Chapter 2 to make sure I was on the right track and for your shared passion and high expectations when it comes to all things printed pattern in education – I cherish our pattern discussions always.

Many thanks to Hilary Carlisle for encouraging the writing over the last three years and for the reassuring read-through at a time it all felt impossible.

To all the contributors, THANK YOU for your generosity and support in filling these pages with your skill and creativity, for putting up with my many email and telephone requests that have enabled me to share your practice insights and design processes.

Finally, writing the book would never have occurred to me without working with the hundreds of design students across Central Saint Martins, Birmingham City University and Norwich University of the Arts since 1999, some included in these pages. It has been a delight! Thank you, I am indebted – each tutorial insight, design approach, challenge and success has contributed to my own learning and understanding of this subject.

The publishers would like to thank Shirley Mclauchlan and Elizabeth Shorrock for their very helpful feedback on the manuscript.

IMAGE CREDITS

Chapter 3

Conclusion